CONGRESSIONAL POLICIES, PRACTICES AND PROCEDURES

DISTRIBUTION OF HOUSEHOLD INCOME AND FEDERAL TAXES

2008-2010

CONGRESSIONAL POLICIES, PRACTICES AND PROCEDURES

Additional books in this series can be found on Nova's website under the Series tab.

Additional e-books in this series can be found on Nova's website under the e-book tab.

Congressional Policies, Practices and Procedures

Distribution of Household Income and Federal Taxes 2008-2010

Travis Honeyfield
Editor

New York

Library of Congress Cataloging-in-Publication Data

ISBN: 978-1-63117-264-9

Published by Nova Science Publishers, Inc. † New York

CONTENTS

PREFACE

In this book, the Congressional Budget Office (CBO) extends its estimates of the distribution of household income and federal taxes through 2008 and 2009, the lat¬est year for which comprehensive data are available, and compares those estimates with estimates for 2007 and for the 1979–2009 period. This book also presents the CBO's estimates of the distribution of household income and federal taxes in 2010, and it compares those estimates with estimates for the preceding three decades. Furthermore, this book discusses the effects of changes in tax rules on the distribution of federal taxes in 2013.

Chapter 1 - The recent recession has had a substantial impact on income, the amount of taxes owed, and average tax rates. In this report, the Congressional Budget Office (CBO) extends its estimates of the distribution of household income and federal taxes through 2008 and 2009, the latest year for which comprehensive data are available, and compares those estimates with estimates for 2007 and for the 1979–2009 period.

Chapter 2 - The increase in the nation's economic activity in 2010 affected households' income, federal tax liabilities, and federal tax rates. In this report, the Congressional Budget Office (CBO) presents its estimates of the distribution of household income and federal taxes in 2010, and it compares those estimates with estimates for the preceding three decades. The report also discusses the effects of changes in tax rules on the distribution of federal taxes in 2013.

In: Distribution of Household Income … ISBN: 978-1-63117-264-9
Editor: Travis Honeyfield

Chapter 1

THE DISTRIBUTION OF HOUSEHOLD INCOME AND FEDERAL TAXES, 2008 AND 2009[*]

Edward Harris

NOTES AND DEFINITIONS

Numbers in the text, tables, and figures may not add up to totals because of rounding. Unless otherwise indicated, all years referred to in this study are calendar years. Some of the figures have white vertical bars that indicate the duration of recessions. (A recession extends from the peak of a business cycle to its trough.)

Before-tax income is the sum of market income and government transfers.

Market income is composed of labor income, business income, capital gains, capital income (excluding capital gains), income received in retirement for past services, and other sources of income.

Government transfers are cash payments and in-kind benefits from social insurance and other government assistance programs.

After-tax income is the sum of market income and government transfers, minus federal tax liabilities.

---

[*] Edward Harris wrote this report which was released by the Congressional Budget Office, July 2012.

Federal tax liabilities are the amount of federal taxes a household owes based on income earned in a year, regardless of when the taxes are paid. In assessments of the impact of various taxes, individual income taxes are allocated directly to households paying those taxes. Social insurance, or payroll, taxes are allocated to households paying those taxes directly or paying them indirectly through their employers. Corporate income taxes are allocated to households according to their shares of capital and labor income. Excise taxes are allocated to households according to their consumption of the taxed good or service.

Average federal tax rates are calculated by dividing federal tax liabilities by before-tax income. Negative average tax rates result when refundable tax credits, such as the earned income and child tax credits, exceed the tax owed by people in an income group. (Refundable tax credits are not limited to the amount of income tax owed before they are applied.)

Income categories are defined by ranking all people by their income adjusted for household size—that is, divided by the square root of a household's size. (A household consists of the people who share a housing unit, regardless of their relationships.) Quintiles, or fifths, contain equal numbers of people, as do percentiles, or hundredths. Households with negative income (business or investment losses larger than other income) are excluded from the lowest income category but are included in totals.

Income is adjusted for inflation using the personal consumption expenditures price index, which is calculated by the Bureau of Economic Analysis. These terms are explained in greater detail in the appendix.

SUMMARY

The recent recession has had a substantial impact on income, the amount of taxes owed, and average tax rates. In this report, the Congressional Budget Office (CBO) extends its estimates of the distribution of household income and federal taxes through 2008 and 2009, the latest year for which comprehensive data are available, and compares those estimates with estimates for 2007 and for the 1979–2009 period. Major findings are as follows:

- **Before-Tax Income.** In 2009, the share of total before-tax income (which includes government transfer payments, such as Social Security benefits) received by households in the lowest income quintile (that is, the lowest one-fifth) was 5.1 percent, the share received by households in the middle quintile was 14.7 percent, and the share received by households in the highest quintile was 50.8 percent (see Summary Table 1).[1] Average before-tax income fell 12 percent from 2007 to 2009 in real (inflation-adjusted) terms. The declines in before-tax income were 5 percent or less for households in each of the four lowest income quintiles and 18 percent for households in the top quintile (including a 36 percent decline for households in the top percentile, or top 1 percent). Because income fell more rapidly for households in the top percentile than for other income groups, their share of before-tax income also fell, by 5.3 percentage points.

- **Tax Rates**. Average tax rates depend on tax laws and economic conditions. The average federal tax rate— that is, households' federal tax liabilities divided by their income (including transfer payments) before taxes—was 17.4 percent in 2009 for all households and ranged from 1.0 percent for households in the lowest quintile to 23.2 percent for households in the highest quintile (and to 28.9 percent for households in the top percentile). The average federal tax rate for all households fell 2.5 percentage points from 2007 to 2009, reaching the lowest level seen in the 1979–2009 period. The largest decline was for households in the lowest income quintile. With the decline in before-tax income offset in part by the decrease in federal taxes, average after-tax income fell 10 percent in real terms.
- **Share of Tax Liabilities.** In 2009, the share of federal taxes owed was 0.3 percent for households in the lowest income quintile, 9.4 percent for households in the middle quintile, and 67.9 percent for those in the highest quintile. Declines in before-tax income among households in the top income percentile lowered their share of federal tax liabilities from 26.7 percent to 22.3 percent between 2007 and 2009.

Although the detailed data that form the basis of CBO's estimates in this report are available only through 2009, other data can provide some insight into changes in the distribution of income and federal taxes in 2010 and 2011. Those data suggest that overall income continued to grow slowly in 2010 and 2011 and that income for households toward the higher end of the distribution increased more rapidly than income for households elsewhere in the income distribution in 2010. Average federal tax rates probably remained near their post-1979 low levels in both 2010 and 2011.

Summary Table 1. Distribution of Federal Taxes and Household Income, by Income Group, 2007 and 2009

	Lowest Quintile	Second Quintile	Middle Quintile	Fourth Quintile	Highest Quintile	Quintiles All	81st to 90th Percentiles	91st to 95th Percentiles	96th to 99th Percentiles	Top 1 Percent
	2009									
All Federal Taxes (Percent)										
Average federal tax rate	1.0	6.8	11.1	15.1	23.2	17.4	18.8	21.1	24.1	28.9
Share of tax liabilities	0.3	3.8	9.4	18.3	67.9	100.0	16.1	12.2	17.3	22.3
Income										
Average (2009 dollars)										
Before-tax	23,500	43,400	64,300	93,800	223,500	88,400	131,700	175,800	271,800	1,219,700
After-tax	23,300	40,500	57,100	79,600	171,600	73,100	107,000	138,700	206,200	866,700
Share (Percent)										
Before-tax	5.1	9.8	14.7	21.1	50.8	100.0	14.9	10.1	12.5	13.4
After-tax	6.2	11.1	15.8	21.6	47.2	100.0	14.6	9.6	11.4	11.5
	2007									
All Federal Taxes (Percent)										
Average federal tax rate	5.1	10.3	14.0	17.5	24.7	19.9	20.6	22.5	25.4	28.3
Share of tax liabilities	1.2	4.7	9.4	16.8	67.8	100.0	14.2	10.7	16.2	26.7
Income										
Average (2009 dollars)										
Before-tax	23,900	45,600	67,600	98,400	273,000	101,000	138,000	187,300	315,800	1,917,200
After-tax	22,700	40,800	58,100	81,200	205,600	80,900	109,600	145,200	235,700	1,373,700
Share (Percent)										
Before-tax	4.8	9.0	13.3	19.1	54.6	100.0	13.7	9.5	12.7	18.7
After-tax	5.6	10.0	14.3	19.6	51.4	100.0	13.6	9.2	11.8	16.7
	Change from 2007 to 2009									
Change in All Federal Taxes										
(Percentage points)										
Average federal tax rate	-4.1	-3.5	-2.9	-2.4	-1.5	-2.5	-1.8	-1.4	-1.3	0.6

	Lowest Quintile	Second Quintile	Middle Quintile	Fourth Quintile	Highest Quintile	Quintiles All	81st to 90th Percentiles	91st to 95th Percentiles	96th to 99th Percentiles	Top 1 Percent
Share of tax liabilities	-0.9	-0.9	*	1.5	0.1	0	1.9	1.5	1.1	-4.4
Change in Income										
Average (2009 dollars)										
Before-tax	-400	-2,200	-3,300	-4,600	-49,500	-12,600	-6,300	-11,500	-44,000	-697,500
After-tax	600	-300	-1,000	-1,600	-34,000	-7,800	-2,600	-6,500	-29,500	-507,000
Share (Percentage points)										
Before-tax	0.3	0.8	1.4	2.0	-3.8	0	1.2	0.6	-0.2	-5.3
After-tax	0.6	1.1	1.5	2.0	-4.2	0	1.0	0.4	-0.4	-5.2
Percentage Change in										
Average Income, 2007 to 2009										
Average before-tax income	-2	-5	-5	-5	-18	-12	-5	-6	-14	-36
Average after-tax income	3	-1	-2	-2	-17	-10	-2	-4	-13	-37

Source: Congressional Budget Office.

Notes: Average tax rates are calculated by dividing tax liabilities by before-tax income.

Before-tax income is the sum of market income and government transfers. Market income is composed of labor income, business income, capital gains, capital income (excluding capital gains), income received in retirement for past services, and other sources of income.

Government transfers are cash payments and in-kind benefits from social insurance and other government assistance programs. For more detailed definitions of income, see the appendix.

After-tax income is the sum of market income and government transfers, minus federal tax liabilities.

Quintiles, or fifths, are created by ranking households by their before-tax income. Quintiles contain equal numbers of people.

Federal taxes include individual and corporate income taxes, social insurance (or payroll) taxes, and excise taxes.

Income amounts have been rounded to the nearest $100. *=between -0.05 percentage points and zero.

The analysis in this report reflects two significant changes CBO has made to the methodology it uses to derive estimates of before-tax income and federal tax liability. Specifically, the agency has revised its assumptions about the incidence of the corporate income tax and its method for valuing government-provided health insurance. Those changes are discussed later in the report. CBO has also changed the index it uses to measure inflation; it now uses the personal consumption expenditures (PCE) price index, also referred to as the PCE deflator.

INTRODUCTION

In this analysis, the Congressional Budget Office (CBO) examines the distribution of household income and federal taxes, focusing on calendar years 2008 and 2009. This study builds on the work in previous CBO publications that looked at income and taxes over the 1979–2007 period.[1]

Using data from the Internal Revenue Service (IRS) and survey data collected by the Census Bureau, CBO estimated income—including government transfer payments and federal taxes—for a representative sample of households in each year during that period. (The appendix contains a more detailed discussion of the data and methodology.) This report shows average tax rates for various income categories for the four largest sources of federal revenue—individual income taxes, social insurance (or payroll) taxes, corporate income taxes, and excise taxes— and for the four taxes combined. The report also presents average household income (before and after taxes) and shares of federal taxes and income for each fifth (or quintile) of the income distribution and for subgroups of the top quintile.

The study uses several measures of income. Market income is composed of labor income, business income, capital gains, capital income (excluding capital gains), income received in retirement for past services, and other sources of income. (Labor income includes the value of income received in-kind from sources such as employer-paid health insurance premiums; business income includes taxes paid by businesses that are imputed to households.) Before-tax income is the sum of market income and government transfers, and after-tax income is before-tax income minus federal tax liabilities.

The analysis focuses on annual income, showing average income in different years for different households grouped by income. The households in any particular segment of the income distribution in 2009 were not necessarily the same households who were in that segment in earlier years. The analysis does not assess trends in the distribution of other measures of economic well-being, such as household income measured over a longer period, household consumption, or household wealth. The analysis presents average income and tax rates for various income groups. Within each income group there is considerable variation in income, taxes paid, and tax rates, but this report does not examine that variation.

ESTIMATES FOR 2008 AND 2009

Changes in households' before-tax income and average tax rates in 2008 and 2009 were substantial and differed markedly across the income distribution. Average after-tax income fell notably, owing to a drop in market income that was caused by the recession that began in December 2007 and was only partially offset by increases in government transfers and decreases in federal taxes.

Households' before-Tax Income

Market income is very unevenly distributed. In 2009, households in the lowest income quintile received 2.2 percent of market income, equal to about $7,600 per household, and those in the middle quintile received 13.5 percent, or $54,200 per household (see Table 1 on page 4). Households in the highest quintile received 56.8 percent of income, or $218,800 per household, but that average masks wide differences between subgroups of that quintile; households in the 81st to 90th percentiles received $125,800, on average, compared with $1.2 million for households in the top percentile. This analysis does not separately examine subgroups of the top percentile.

Aggregate market income declined in both 2008 and 2009, largely because of the recession that began in December 2007 and lasted through June 2009 and the slow recovery that followed. Declines were especially steep for capital gains, which fell by 75 percent in real (inflation-adjusted) terms between 2007 and 2009. Other sources of capital income also fell: interest income by 40 percent and dividend income by 33 percent. Wages, the largest source of income, fell by a more modest 6 percent. Average real market income fell by 16 percent between 2007 and 2009.[2]

That decline in market income was mitigated somewhat by an increase in government transfers. Payments from most government transfer programs grew: Transfers rose by 15 percent for Social Security, nearly tripled for unemployment insurance, nearly doubled for the Supplemental Nutrition Assistance Program, and grew by between 5 percent and 10 percent for Medicare and Medicaid. Consequently, real before-tax income fell by 12 percent, less than the 16 percent decline in market income alone.

Government transfers lift incomes for all income groups, but the increases are larger for households with less income. In 2009, households in the bottom quintile of the market-income distribution received over 40 percent of total transfer payments—an average of about $23,000 per household. Almost two-thirds of that came from Social Security and Medicare. The share of transfers received fell steadily moving up the income distribution, with the top quintile receiving less than 10 percent of transfer payments. (Higher-income households receive transfers because eligibility for some large programs, such as Social Security and Medicare, is not based on household income.)

Because of that pattern, before-tax income is more evenly distributed than is market income alone. Households in the lowest quintile of the before-tax income distribution received 5.1 percent of income, the middle quintile received 14.7 percent, and the top quintile received 50.8 percent.

Federal Tax Rates

Decreases in federal taxes meant that the drop in after-tax income was also less than the decline in market income. The overall average federal tax rate (household federal tax liabilities divided by before-tax household income) declined from 19.9 percent of income in 2007 to 18.0 percent in 2008 and 17.4 percent in 2009 (see Table 2 on page 6).

The average individual income tax rate (household income tax liabilities divided by before-tax household income) fell to 7.2 percent in 2009—a drop of 2.0 percentage points from 2007—owing to both declines in income and changes in tax law. The average social insurance tax rate (household payroll tax liabilities divided by before-tax household income) rose 0.7 percentage points, to 8.0 percent of household income in 2009. That average rate rose because earnings fell by less than did other sources of income and because earnings above the cap on payroll taxes ($106,800 in 2009) fell more rapidly than did earnings below it.

The average individual income tax rate is typically higher than the payroll tax rate, but in 2009 it was lower. Two factors explain that unusual result. First, because the tax base for payroll taxes is limited to earnings, a steep drop in nonwage income (such as interest, dividends, and capital gains) reduced income taxes but not payroll taxes in 2009. Second, the American Recovery and Reinvestment Act of 2009 (ARRA, Public Law 111-5) made several changes that lowered individual income taxes in that year. The act introduced new refundable income tax credits and expanded existing ones. In the analysis for this report, CBO measured individual income taxes net of refundable credits.[3]

The average corporate income tax rate (corporate taxes allocated to households divided by before-tax household income) also fell between 2007 and 2009—by 1.4 percentage points, to a rate of 1.5 percent in 2009. That change reflects both a sharp decline in corporate profits in 2008 that was only partially reversed in 2009 and legislation that reduced corporate income taxes in both 2008 and 2009. Excise taxes averaged 0.6 percent of household income in 2009, up 0.1 percentage point from 2007.

Distribution of Federal Taxes across the Income Scale

The federal tax system is progressive—that is, average tax rates generally rise with income. In 2009, households in the bottom fifth of the before-tax income distribution paid 1.0 percent of their before-tax income in federal taxes, households in the middle quintile paid 11.1 percent, and households in the highest quintile paid 23.2 percent (see Figure 1 on page 8). Average rates were higher for higher-income groups within the top quintile, and households in the top 1 percent of the before-tax income distribution faced an average rate of 28.9 percent.

Because average federal tax rates rise with income, the share of federal taxes paid by higher-income households exceeded their share of before-tax income, and the opposite was true for lower-income households. In 2009, households in the highest quintile received 50.8 percent of before-tax income and paid 67.9 percent of federal taxes; households in the top 1 percent received 13.4 percent of income and paid 22.3 percent of taxes (see Figure 2 on page 9). In all other quintiles, the share of federal taxes paid was smaller than the share of before-tax income: Households in the bottom quintile received 5.1 percent of income and paid 0.3 percent of taxes, and households in the middle quintile received 14.7 percent of income and paid 9.4 percent of taxes.

Individual Income Taxes

Much of the progressivity of the federal tax system derives from the individual income tax. In 2009, the bottom quintile's average rate for the individual income tax was -9.3 percent—that is, refundable tax credits exceeded the income tax owed by that group (see Figure 3 on page 10). On average, households in the second quintile also received more in refundable credits than they paid in individual income taxes. The average income tax rate was 1.3 percent for the middle quintile, 4.6 percent for the fourth quintile, and 13.4 percent for the highest quintile. The top 1 percent, on average, paid 21.0 percent of their income in individual income taxes. Two changes in tax law lowered individual income tax rates in 2008 and 2009 relative to what they were in 2007. The Economic Stimulus Act of 2008 (P.L. 110- 185) provided a partially refundable payment of between $300 and $600 per person in 2008.[4] Several provisions of ARRA reduced individual income taxes in 2009. The largest tax provision was the Making Work Pay credit, a refundable credit of up to $400 for a single worker or $800 for a married couple. Other provisions of ARRA increased the exemption for the alternative minimum tax, provided special additional payments for Social Security beneficiaries, lowered the threshold for the refundable child tax credit, created the American Opportunity Tax Credit (a new credit for college expenses), expanded the earned income tax credit, and exempted some unemployment compensation from individual income taxes.

The changes in tax law reduced average tax rates more for lower-income taxpayers than for higher-income taxpayers, primarily because of the Making Work Pay credit, which phased out for taxpayers with higher income. Between 2007 and 2009, the individual income tax rate fell by more than 3 percentage points for the lowest income quintile, about 2.5 points for the second quintile, just under 2 points for the middle quintile, roughly 1.5 points for the fourth quintile, and about 1 point for the top quintile. In contrast, the average rate for households in the top percentile rose. The reason is that capital gains and dividends, which are taxed at preferential rates below the rates on other taxable income, fell by much more than other sources of income, and capital gains and dividends are a much larger portion of income for households in the top percentile than for those in other income groups.

The changes in average individual income tax rates between 2007 and 2009 led to a larger share of income taxes being paid by households who were higher in the income distribution. Specifically, between 2007 and 2009, the share of taxes paid fell for the bottom three income quintiles, was close to flat for the fourth quintile, but rose for the highest quintile (from 86 percent to 94 percent). Within the top quintile, however, the shift was uneven; the share paid by the top percentile fell, and the share paid by the rest of the top quintile rose.

Table 1. Distribution of Before-Tax Income, by Income Group, 2007 to 2009

Income Group	With Households Ranked by Market Income			With Households Ranked by Before-Tax Income
	Market Income	Transfers Received	Before-Tax Income	
	Average Income (2009 dollars)[a]			
	2009			
Lowest Quintile	7,600	22,900	30,500	23,500
Second Quintile	30,100	14,800	45,000	43,400
Middle Quintile	54,200	10,400	64,600	64,300
Fourth Quintile	86,400	7,100	93,500	93,800
Highest Quintile	218,800	6,000	224,800	223,500
All Quintiles	75,700	12,700	88,400	88,400
81st to 90th Percentiles	125,800	5,800	131,600	131,700
91st to 95th Percentiles	169,800	5,700	175,500	175,800
96th to 99th Percentiles	266,200	6,200	272,400	271,800
Top 1 Percent	1,219,600	9,000	1,228,600	1,219,700
	2008			
Lowest Quintile	8,900	20,300	29,200	23,500
Second Quintile	33,100	12,300	45,500	43,800
Middle Quintile	57,100	8,500	65,600	65,400
Fourth Quintile	89,800	6,100	95,900	95,700
Highest Quintile	243,200	5,400	248,700	246,600
All Quintiles	82,600	11,000	93,600	93,600
81st to 90th Percentiles	130,000	5,100	135,100	135,000
91st to 95th Percentiles	175,900	5,300	181,200	180,500
96th to 99th Percentiles	286,800	5,800	292,600	290,500
Top 1 Percent	1,559,900	9,000	1,568,900	1,558,900
	2007			
Lowest Quintile	9,900	19,700	29,600	23,900
Second Quintile	35,200	12,000	47,100	45,600
Middle Quintile	59,800	8,200	68,000	67,600
Fourth Quintile	92,500	6,100	98,600	98,400
Highest Quintile	269,400	6,000	275,400	273,000
All Quintiles	90,300	10,800	101,000	101,000
81st to 90th Percentiles	132,800	5,300	138,200	138,000
91st to 95th Percentiles	182,300	5,700	187,900	187,300
96th to 99th Percentiles	310,700	7,200	317,900	315,800
Top 1 Percent	1,919,700	9,400	1,929,100	1,917,200

Table 1. (Continued)

Income Group	With Households Ranked by Market Income			With Households Ranked by Before-Tax Income
	Market Income	Transfers Received	Before-Tax Income	
	Share of Income (Percent) 2009			
Lowest Quintile	2.2	40.5	7.7	5.1
Second Quintile	7.6	22.4	9.7	9.8
Middle Quintile	13.5	15.5	13.8	14.7
Fourth Quintile	21.7	10.7	20.1	21.1
Highest Quintile	56.8	9.3	50.0	50.8
All Quintiles	100.0	100.0	100.0	100.0
81st to 90th Percentiles	16.2	4.4	14.5	14.9
91st to 95th Percentiles	11.1	2.2	9.9	10.1
96th to 99th Percentiles	14.1	2.0	12.4	12.5
Top 1 Percent	15.4	0.7	13.3	13.4
	2008			
Lowest Quintile	2.5	42.3	7.1	5.0
Second Quintile	7.6	21.4	9.2	9.4
Middle Quintile	13.0	14.5	13.2	13.9
Fourth Quintile	20.5	10.5	19.3	20.1
Highest Quintile	57.8	9.8	52.1	52.8
All Quintiles	100.0	100.0	100.0	100.0
81st to 90th Percentiles	15.2	4.5	14.0	14.3
91st to 95th Percentiles	10.6	2.4	9.7	9.8
96th to 99th Percentiles	13.9	2.1	12.5	12.6
Top 1 Percent	18.0	0.8	16.0	16.0
	2007			
Lowest Quintile	2.5	41.7	6.7	4.8
Second Quintile	7.4	21.1	8.9	9.0
Middle Quintile	12.5	14.3	12.7	13.3
Fourth Quintile	19.3	10.6	18.4	19.1
Highest Quintile	59.2	11.0	54.1	54.6
All Quintiles	100.0	100.0	100.0	100.0
81st to 90th Percentiles	14.5	4.9	13.4	13.7
91st to 95th Percentiles	10.1	2.6	9.3	9.5
96th to 99th Percentiles	13.8	2.7	12.6	12.7
Top 1 Percent	20.8	0.9	18.7	18.7

Source: Congressional Budget Office.

Notes: Market income is composed of labor income, business income, capital gains, capital income (excluding capital gains), income received in retirement for past services, and other sources of income. Government transfers are cash payments and in-kind benefits from social insurance and other government assistance programs. Before-tax income is the sum of market income and government transfers.

For more detailed definitions of income, see the appendix.

Quintiles, or fifths, are created by ranking households by either their market or before-tax income. Quintiles contain equal numbers of people.

a. Income amounts have been rounded to the nearest $100.

Table 2. Distribution of Federal Taxes, by Income Group, 2007 to 2009

Before-Tax Income Group	All Federal Taxes	Individual Income Taxes	Social Insurance Taxes	Corporate Income Taxes	Excise Taxes
	Average Federal Tax Rate (Percentage of before-tax income)				
	2009				
Lowest Quintile	1.0	-9.3	8.3	0.5	1.5
Second Quintile	6.8	-2.6	7.9	0.5	0.9
Middle Quintile	11.1	1.3	8.4	0.6	0.8
Fourth Quintile	15.1	4.6	9.1	0.7	0.6
Highest Quintile	23.2	13.4	7.2	2.3	0.4
All Quintiles	17.4	7.2	8.0	1.5	0.6
81st to 90th Percentiles	18.8	7.7	9.7	0.9	0.5
91st to 95th Percentiles	21.1	10.3	9.2	1.1	0.5
96th to 99th Percentiles	24.1	14.6	7.4	1.7	0.4
Top 1 Percent	28.9	21.0	2.5	5.2	0.2
	2008				
Lowest Quintile	1.5	-9.1	8.6	0.6	1.3
Second Quintile	7.3	-2.5	8.3	0.6	0.9
Middle Quintile	11.6	1.2	8.9	0.8	0.7
Fourth Quintile	15.6	4.7	9.4	0.9	0.6
Highest Quintile	23.6	14.0	6.5	2.7	0.4
All Quintiles	18.0	7.8	7.8	1.8	0.6
81st to 90th Percentiles	19.1	7.9	9.6	1.1	0.5
91st to 95th Percentiles	21.7	10.8	9.1	1.4	0.4
96th to 99th Percentiles	24.7	15.4	6.8	2.1	0.4
Top 1 Percent	28.1	20.4	2.0	5.5	0.2
	2007				
Lowest Quintile	5.1	-5.8	8.7	1.0	1.2
Second Quintile	10.3	-0.1	8.6	1.0	0.8
Middle Quintile	14.0	3.1	8.9	1.3	0.7
Fourth Quintile	17.5	6.1	9.3	1.5	0.6
Highest Quintile	24.7	14.4	5.8	4.1	0.3
All Quintiles	19.9	9.2	7.3	2.9	0.5
81st to 90th Percentiles	20.6	8.9	9.4	1.8	0.5
91st to 95th Percentiles	22.5	11.2	8.5	2.3	0.4

Table 2. (Continued)

Before-Tax Income Group	All Federal Taxes	Individual Income Taxes	Social Insurance Taxes	Corporate Income Taxes	Excise Taxes
			2007		
96th to 99th Percentiles	25.4	15.5	6.0	3.5	0.3
Top 1 Percent	28.3	19.4	1.6	7.2	0.1
	Share of Federal Tax Liabilities (Percent)				
			2009		
Lowest Quintile	0.3	-6.6	5.3	1.8	12.2
Second Quintile	3.8	-3.5	9.7	3.2	15.1
Middle Quintile	9.4	2.7	15.4	5.8	18.8
Fourth Quintile	18.3	13.4	24.0	10.2	21.3
Highest Quintile	67.9	94.1	45.3	77.2	32.1
All Quintiles	100.0	100.0	100.0	100.0	100.0
81st to 90th Percentiles	16.1	15.9	17.9	8.7	12.5
91st to 95th Percentiles	12.2	14.3	11.6	7.4	7.5
96th to 99th Percentiles	17.3	25.2	11.6	14.1	7.7
Top 1 Percent	22.3	38.7	4.2	47.1	4.4
			2008		
Lowest Quintile	0.4	-5.8	5.5	1.7	11.9
Second Quintile	3.8	-3.0	10.0	3.2	14.6
Middle Quintile	8.9	2.2	15.8	5.7	18.1
Fourth Quintile	17.4	12.1	24.3	9.9	20.9
Highest Quintile	69.2	94.6	44.1	78.0	34.1
All Quintiles	100.0	100.0	100.0	100.0	100.0
81st to 90th Percentiles	15.1	14.5	17.6	8.5	12.6
91st to 95th Percentiles	11.8	13.5	11.4	7.3	7.7
96th to 99th Percentiles	17.3	24.8	11.0	14.4	8.1
Top 1 Percent	25.0	41.8	4.2	47.8	5.7
			2007		
Lowest Quintile	1.2	-3.0	5.6	1.7	10.9
Second Quintile	4.7	-0.1	10.5	3.2	14.2
Middle Quintile	9.4	4.6	16.2	5.8	18.3
Fourth Quintile	16.8	12.6	24.4	9.9	22.2
Highest Quintile	67.8	86.0	43.1	78.5	34.2
All Quintiles	100.0	100.0	100.0	100.0	100.0
81st to 90th Percentiles	14.2	13.3	17.6	8.6	13.5
91st to 95th Percentiles	10.7	11.6	11.1	7.7	7.9

Before-Tax	All Federal	Individual	Social	Corporate	Excise
Income Group	Taxes	Income Taxes	Insurance Taxes	Income Taxes	Taxes
			2007		
96th to 99th Percentiles	16.2	21.5	10.4	15.6	8.0
Top 1 Percent	26.7	39.6	4.1	46.7	4.8

Source: Congressional Budget Office.

Notes: Average tax rates are calculated by dividing tax liabilities of each type by total before-tax income for each income group.

Before-tax income is the sum of market income and government transfers. Market income is composed of labor income, business income, capital gains, capital income (excluding capital gains), income received in retirement for past services, and other sources of income. Government transfers are cash payments and in-kind benefits from social insurance and other government assistance programs. For more detailed definitions of income, see the appendix.

Quintiles, or fifths, are created by ranking households by their before-tax income. Quintiles contain equal numbers of people.

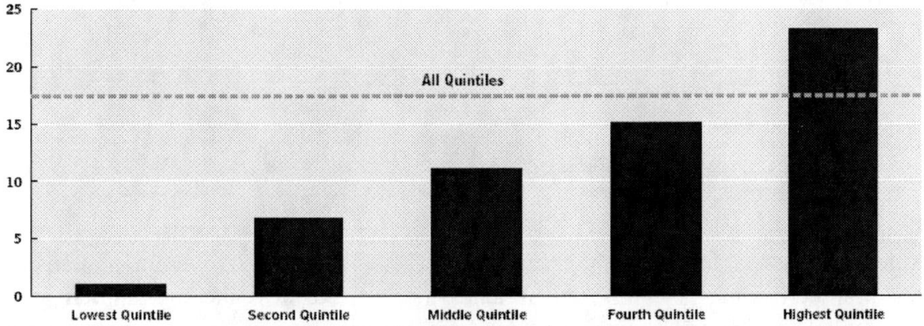

Notes: Average tax rates are calculated by dividing tax liabilities by before-tax income.

Before-tax income is the sum of market income and government transfers. Market income is composed of labor income, business income, capital gains, capital income (excluding capital gains), income received in retirement for past services, and other sources of income. Government transfers are cash payments and in-kind benefits from social insurance and other government assistance programs. For more detailed definitions of income, see the appendix.

Quintiles, or fifths, are created by ranking households by their before-tax income. Quintiles contain equal numbers of people. Federal taxes include individual and corporate income taxes, social insurance (or payroll) taxes, and excise taxes.

Figure 1. Average Federal Tax Rates, by Income Group, 2009; (Percent).

Social Insurance (Payroll) Taxes

Average rates for payroll taxes are fairly flat across most of the income distribution but are lower at the top. In 2009, the average payroll tax rate was 8.3 percent for the lowest quintile, 7.9 percent for the second quintile, 8.4 percent for the middle quintile, and 9.1 percent for the fourth quintile, compared with 7.2 percent for the highest quintile and 2.5 percent for the top percentile of households (see Table 2 on page 6). The rate for higher-income households is lower than that for others in part because more of the earnings for those households are above the maximum income subject to Social Security taxes and in part because earnings are a smaller share of their income. Social insurance taxes account for the largest share of taxes paid by households in all but the top quintile.

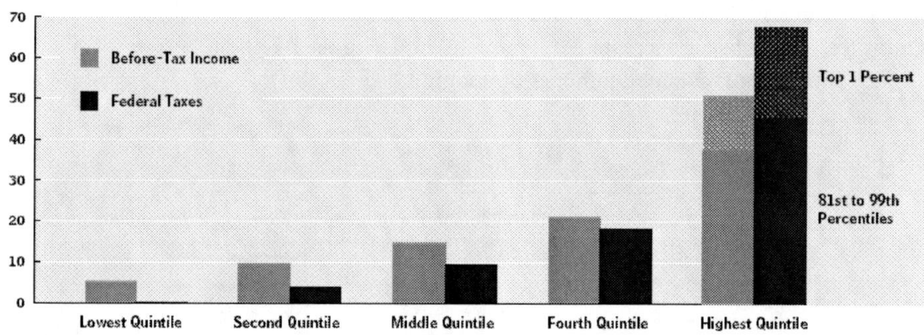

Source: Congressional Budget Office.

Notes: Before-tax income is the sum of market income and government transfers. Market income is composed of labor income, business income, capital gains, capital income (excluding capital gains), income received in retirement for past services, and other sources of income. Government transfers are cash payments and in-kind benefits from social insurance and other government assistance programs. For more detailed definitions of income, see the appendix.

Quintiles, or fifths, are created by ranking households by their before-tax income. Quintiles contain equal numbers of people. Federal taxes include individual and corporate income taxes, social insurance (or payroll) taxes, and excise taxes.

Figure 2. Shares of Before-Tax Income and Federal Taxes, by Income Group, 2009; (Percent).

The average social insurance tax rate (social insurance taxes as a share of before-tax income) rose between 2007 and 2009, from 7.3 percent to 8.0 percent. Aggregate payroll tax rates increased because wages and salaries—the base for the tax—fell more slowly than did other types of income, pushing up payroll taxes as a share of total income. Also, wages of taxpayers whose earnings were above the taxable maximum fell by more than wages of taxpayers whose earnings were below it. Consequently, the share of wages subject to the Social Security payroll tax rose, pushing up the average tax rate.

The pattern of changes was not uniform across the income distribution, however. Average payroll tax rates decreased for the bottom three quintiles; for those groups, wages declined as a share of total income, because government transfers rose and wages fell. In contrast, the rate for the highest quintile rose by 1.4 percentage points, because wages fell by less than did income from sources not subject to the payroll tax.

Corporate Income Taxes

The impact of the federal corporate income tax also rises with income, because CBO assumed in this analysis that most of the tax is borne by capital income, which is a larger share of income at the top of the distribution. Under CBO's assumption, the highest income quintile paid almost 80 percent of the corporate income tax during the 2007– 2009 period. In 2009, the average corporate income tax rate (corporate taxes as a share of before-tax household income) was 0.5 percent for the lowest quintile, 0.6 percent for the middle quintile, and 2.3 percent for the highest quintile. The average rate fell between 2007 and 2009, from 2.9 percent to 1.5 percent. Higher-income groups experienced a larger percentage-point decline in the tax.

Excise Taxes

The effect of federal excise taxes, relative to income, is greatest for lower-income households, who tend to spend a large share of their income on such goods as gasoline, alcohol, and tobacco, which are subject to such taxes. Average excise tax rates changed little between 2007 and 2009, however—no more than three-tenths of a percentage point for any income group.

Households' after-Tax Income

Average federal tax rates rise with income, causing the distribution of after-tax income to be more even than that of before-tax income.[5] In 2009, households in the bottom four quintiles of the before-tax income distribution each received a share of after-tax income that was about 1 percentage point larger than their share of before-tax income (see Figure 4 on page 11). In contrast, households in the highest quintile received 47.2 percent of after-tax income and 50.8 percent of before-tax income.

Declines in after-tax income between 2007 and 2009 were heavily concentrated at the top of the income distribution (see Table 3 on page 12). After-tax income fell by 37 percent for the top 1 percent of households and by about 5 percent for households in the 81st to 99th percentiles. Households in the middle three quintiles of the income distribution experienced more modest declines (1 percent to 2 percent), and after-tax income increased slightly for households in the lowest quintile. As a consequence of those changes, the share of after-tax income accruing to the top percentile of the distribution fell by 5.2 percentage points. The share earned by each of the bottom four income quintiles rose between 0.6 and 2.0 percentage points, and the share earned by the 81st to 99th percentiles rose 1.0 percentage point.

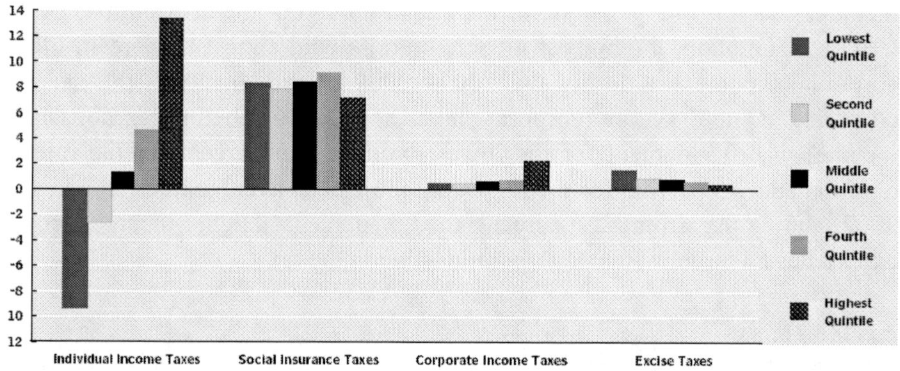

Source: Congressional Budget Office.

Notes: Average tax rates are calculated by dividing tax liabilities of each type by total before-tax income for each income group.

Before-tax income is the sum of market income and government transfers. Market income is composed of labor income, business income, capital gains, capital income (excluding capital gains), income received in retirement for past services, and other sources of income. Government transfers are cash payments and in-kind benefits from social insurance and other government assistance programs. For more detailed definitions of income, see the appendix.

Quintiles, or fifths, are created by ranking households by their before-tax income. Quintiles contain equal numbers of people.

Figure 3. Average Federal Tax Rates, by Income Group and Tax Source, 2009; (Percent).

Changes in the distribution of market income were responsible for much of the shift in the distribution of after-tax income between 2007 and 2009. Large declines in sources of market income that tilt heavily toward high-income households—such as capital gains and interest—caused the large decline in top incomes; for households in the highest percentile, average market income dropped 36 percent between 2007 and 2009.

Although market income was the primary factor causing the shift in the distribution of after-tax income, federal taxes and government transfers also contributed. Transfers were flat, in real terms, for the highest income quintile but rose for all other income groups. And average federal tax rates rose slightly for the top 1 percent of households but fell for all other groups, with the largest decreases experienced by those at the bottom of the income distribution. Thus, the downward shift in the distribution of income after federal taxes and transfers was larger than the downward shift in market income.

HISTORICAL TRENDS

Many of the changes in average federal tax rates and after-tax income in 2008 and 2009 are notable when viewed from a longer historical perspective:

- The overall average federal tax rates of 18.0 percent in 2008 and 17.4 percent in 2009 were the lowest in the 1979–2009 period (see Figure 5 on page 14) and were well below the previous low of 19.4 percent in 2003 and the average of 21.0 percent over that period.
- The average federal individual income tax rate also reached a new low in 2009, at 7.2 percent of household income, falling below previous low marks in 2008 and 2003. The average individual income tax rate fell below the average social insurance tax rate for the first time in the 31 years covered by this analysis.
- The average federal corporate income tax rate also approached the lowest level in the 1979–2009 period.
- The decline in after-tax income for the highest-income households reversed a substantial portion of the sharp rise in their income between 1979 and 2007 (see Figure 6 on page 15).

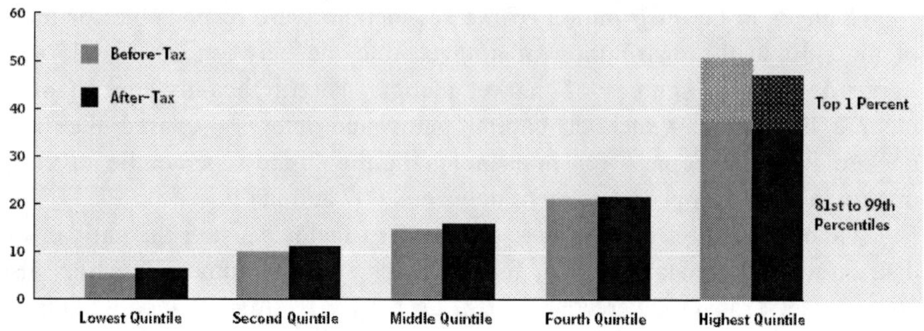

Source: Congressional Budget Office.

Notes: Before-tax income is the sum of market income and government transfers. Market income is composed of labor income, business income, capital gains, capital income (excluding capital gains), income received in retirement for past services, and other sources of income. Government transfers are cash payments and in-kind benefits from social insurance and other government assistance programs.

After-tax income is the sum of market income and government transfers, minus federal tax liabilities.

For more detailed definitions of income, see the appendix.

Quintiles, or fifths, are created by ranking households by their before-tax income. Quintiles contain equal numbers of people. Federal taxes include individual and corporate income taxes, social insurance (or payroll) taxes, and excise taxes.

Figure 4. Shares of Before- and After-Tax Income, by Income Group, 2009; (Percent).

Average Federal Tax Rates, by Source

The 2009 overall average federal tax rate (household tax liabilities divided by before-tax income) was the lowest observed in the 1979–2009 period, falling from 22.0 percent in 1979 to 17.4 percent in 2009 (see the top panel of Figure 5 on page 14). The rate declined in the early 1980s, then rose through much of the 1980s and 1990s. It peaked at 22.7 percent in 2000 and then fell sharply following the 2001 recession and tax legislation enacted in 2001 and 2003, reaching just under 19.4 percent in 2003. The rate rebounded somewhat over the next few years as economic conditions improved, before dropping substantially in 2008 and 2009.

The average individual income tax rate peaked at 11.9 percent of household income in 1981, then fell as the reduction in tax rates enacted in 1981 took effect. Legislation enacted in 1993 and rapidly rising incomes pushed the rate up again in the late 1990s—to 11.7 percent in 2000, close to its highest level. The rate then fell to 8.3 percent in 2003 as a result of the 2001 and 2003 tax cuts and the recession in 2001. Rates fell again in 2008 and 2009, to a new low of 7.2 percent of household income, largely because of declines in income and changes in tax law, as discussed earlier.

The average social insurance tax rate rose from 6.8 percent in 1979 to 8.0 percent in 2009. The rate rose throughout the 1980s because of legislated increases in the cap on earnings subject to the Social Security payroll tax and because of legislation enacted in 1983 that accelerated previously scheduled increases in the Social Security payroll tax rate. Subsequent legislation in the early 1990s first increased and then eliminated the cap on earnings subject to the Hospital Insurance payroll tax (which is used to finance a portion of Medicare). The payroll tax rate declined in the late 1990s and early 2000s as labor income grew more slowly than other income sources and as earnings above the maximum level subject to Social Security taxes grew more rapidly than earnings below that level. Those trends reversed in 2008 and 2009, causing the average payroll tax rate to rise.

Table 3. Distribution of Before- and After-Tax Income and Federal Taxes, by Income Group, 2007 to 2009

Before-Tax Income Group	Before-Tax Income	Federal Tax Liability	After-Tax Income
	Average Amount (2009 dollars)[a]		
	2009		
Lowest Quintile	23,500	200	23,300
Second Quintile	43,400	2,900	40,500
Middle Quintile	64,300	7,200	57,100
Fourth Quintile	93,800	14,100	79,600
Highest Quintile	223,500	51,900	171,600
All Quintiles	88,400	15,300	73,100
81st to 90th Percentiles	131,700	24,700	107,000
91st to 95th Percentiles	175,800	37,000	138,700
96th to 99th Percentiles	271,800	65,600	206,200
Top 1 Percent	1,219,700	353,000	866,700
	2008		
Lowest Quintile	23,500	300	23,200
Second Quintile	43,800	3,200	40,600
Middle Quintile	65,400	7,600	57,900
Fourth Quintile	95,700	14,900	80,700
Highest Quintile	246,600	58,300	188,300
All Quintiles	93,600	16,900	76,700
81st to 90th Percentiles	135,000	25,800	109,200
91st to 95th Percentiles	180,500	39,100	141,400

Table 3. (Continued)

Before-Tax Income Group	Before-Tax Income	Federal Tax Liability	After-Tax Income
		2008	
96th to 99th Percentiles	290,500	71,600	218,900
Top 1 Percent	1,558,900	438,300	1,120,500
		2007	
Lowest Quintile	23,900	1,200	22,700
Second Quintile	45,600	4,700	40,800
Middle Quintile	67,600	9,500	58,100
Fourth Quintile	98,400	17,200	81,200
Highest Quintile	273,000	67,400	205,600
All Quintiles	101,000	20,100	80,900
81st to 90th Percentiles	138,000	28,400	109,600
91st to 95th Percentiles	187,300	42,100	145,200
96th to 99th Percentiles	315,800	80,100	235,700
Top 1 Percent	1,917,200	543,400	1,373,700
		Share of Total Amount (Percent)	
		2009	
Lowest Quintile	5.1	0.3	6.2
Second Quintile	9.8	3.8	11.1
Middle Quintile	14.7	9.4	15.8
Fourth Quintile	21.1	18.3	21.6
Highest Quintile	50.8	67.9	47.2
All Quintiles	100.0	100.0	100.0
81st to 90th Percentiles	14.9	16.1	14.6
91st to 95th Percentiles	10.1	12.2	9.6
96th to 99th Percentiles	12.5	17.3	11.4
Top 1 Percent	13.4	22.3	11.5
		2008	
Lowest Quintile	5.0	0.4	6.0
Second Quintile	9.4	3.8	10.6
Middle Quintile	13.9	8.9	15.0
Fourth Quintile	20.1	17.4	20.7
Highest Quintile	52.8	69.2	49.1
All Quintiles	100.0	100.0	100.0
81st to 90th Percentiles	14.3	15.1	14.1
91st to 95th Percentiles	9.8	11.8	9.4
96th to 99th Percentiles	12.6	17.3	11.6
Top 1 Percent	16.0	25.0	14.1
		2007	
Lowest Quintile	4.8	1.2	5.6
Second Quintile	9.0	4.7	10.0
Middle Quintile	13.3	9.4	14.3
Fourth Quintile	19.1	16.8	19.6
Highest Quintile	54.6	67.8	51.4
All Quintiles	100.0	100.0	100.0

Before-Tax Income Group	Before-Tax Income	Federal Tax Liability	After-Tax Income
		2007	
81st to 90th Percentiles	13.7	14.2	13.6
91st to 95th Percentiles	9.5	10.7	9.2
96th to 99th Percentiles	12.7	16.2	11.8
Top 1 Percent	18.7	26.7	16.7

Source: Congressional Budget Office.

Notes: Before-tax income is the sum of market income and government transfers. Market income is composed of labor income, business income, capital gains, capital income (excluding capital gains), income received in retirement for past services, and other sources of income. Government transfers are cash payments and in-kind benefits from social insurance and other government assistance programs.

After-tax income is the sum of market income and government transfers, minus federal tax liabilities.

For more detailed definitions of income, see the appendix.

Quintiles, or fifths, are created by ranking households by their before-tax income. Quintiles contain equal numbers of people. a. Income amounts have been rounded to the nearest $100.

Average Federal Tax Rates, by Income Group

For most income groups, the 2009 average federal tax rate was the lowest observed in the 1979–2009 period (see the bottom panel of Figure 5). The pattern in the intervening years is more varied, reflecting the interaction of numerous changes to tax law and changes in the composition and distribution of income. For the lowest income group, the average rate fell from 7.5 percent in 1979 to 1.0 percent in 2009. Almost two-thirds of that decline came between 2007 and 2009, largely as a result of new refundable tax credits, as discussed earlier. Declines in earlier years were mainly caused by increases in the earned income tax credit, especially in the 1990s. Payroll tax rates rose steadily for the lowest income group, offsetting some of the decline in their individual income tax rates.

Households in the middle three income quintiles saw their average tax rate fall by 7.1 percentage points over 30 years, from 19.1 percent in 1979 to 12.0 percent in 2009. That decline was due primarily to declines in individual income taxes.

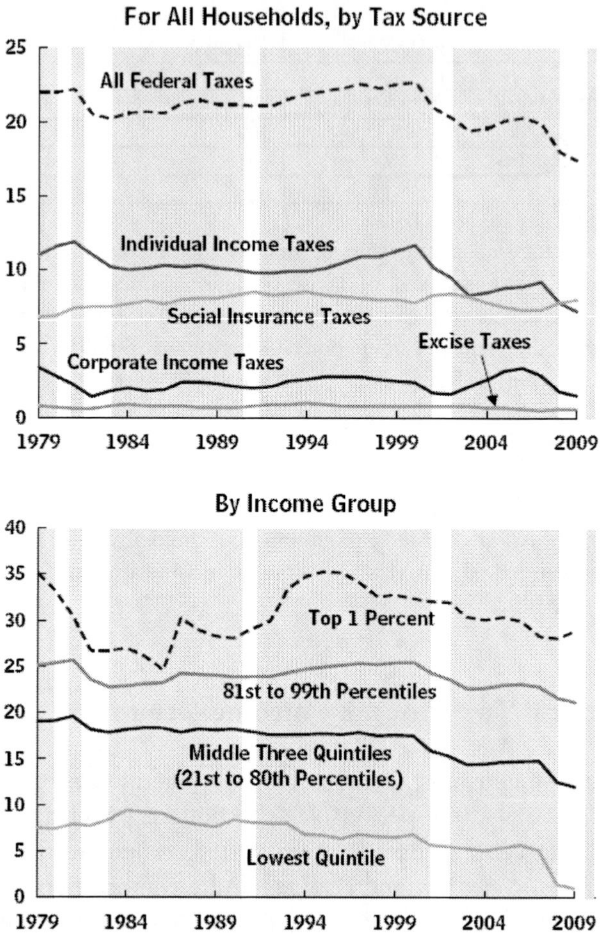

Source: Congressional Budget Office.

Notes: Average tax rates are calculated by dividing tax liabilities of each type by total before-tax income for each income group.

Before-tax income is the sum of market income and government transfers. Market income is composed of labor income, business income, capital gains, capital income (excluding capital gains), income received in retirement for past services, and other sources of income. Government transfers are cash payments and in-kind benefits from social insurance and other government assistance programs. For more detailed definitions of income, see the appendix.

Quintiles, or fifths, are created by ranking households by their before-tax income. Quintiles contain equal numbers of people.

Figure 5. Average Federal Tax Rates, 1979 to 2009; (Percent).

The average tax rate for that group fell somewhat in the early 1980s and then fluctuated within a fairly narrow band through the 1980s and 1990s. Between 2000 and 2003, the rate declined by 3.1 percentage points, reflecting numerous changes in law enacted in 2001—such as the expansion of the child tax credit, reductions in tax rates, and increases in the standard deduction for married couples—that lessened taxes for households in the middle quintiles. The average tax rate on the middle quintiles then rose slightly over the 2003–2007 period, before falling 2.8 percentage points from 2007 to 2009.

The average tax rate for households in the 81st to 99th percentiles of the income distribution also reached a low point in 2009, about 4 percentage points below its 1979 level. That rate fell in the early 1980s and then crept up over the remaining part of that decade and the 1990s, so in 2000 it slightly exceeded its 1979 level. The average tax rate for that group fell 2.9 percentage points between 2000 and 2003, crept up from 2003 to 2007, and then fell another 1.7 percentage points from 2007 to 2009.

In contrast, in 2009 the average tax rate for households in the top 1 percent of the before-tax income distribution was above its low point, reached in the early 1980s. The average tax rate for those households fell in the early 1980s and then rose following enactment of the Tax Reform Act of 1986. The average tax rate for that group then fell somewhat again in the latter half of the 1980s before climbing, on balance, in the 1990s. That upward movement reflected changes in law that raised tax rates for that group as well as rapid increases in their income, which caused their average tax rate to rise as more income was taxed in higher tax brackets. Tax rates for households in the top percentile declined after 2000. The decline was especially rapid in 2003, when a reduction in the tax rate for the top tax bracket enacted in 2001 took effect and further changes in law reduced tax rates on dividends and realized capital gains. The tax rate fell again in 2007, mostly because of declines in corporate income taxes, then rose somewhat from 2007 to 2009, as sharp declines in capital gains income caused a larger portion of the income of that group to be subject to the ordinary income tax rates.

The decline in after-tax income between 2007 and 2009 was much larger at the top of the income distribution than further down the distribution. The decline in income for the highest-income households reversed a substantial portion of the sharp rise in their income between 1979 and 2007 (see Figure 6). The closest historic parallel is the 2001 recession, which, like the most recent recession, was accompanied by a large drop in the value of assets. After-tax income for households in the top percentile of the before-tax income distribution fell 28 percent from 2000 to 2002 and then began growing quickly, surpassing the 2000 level in 2005. Partial evidence, discussed in the next section, indicates that income at the top of the income distribution rebounded somewhat in 2010 from its 2009 level. In prior recessions, declines in income for the highest-income households were less severe than in the two most recent recessions. After-tax income for households in the top 1 percent of the before-tax income distribution fell 15 percent between 1989 and 1991 and, during the recessions of 1980 and 1981–1982, barely fell from its level in 1979.

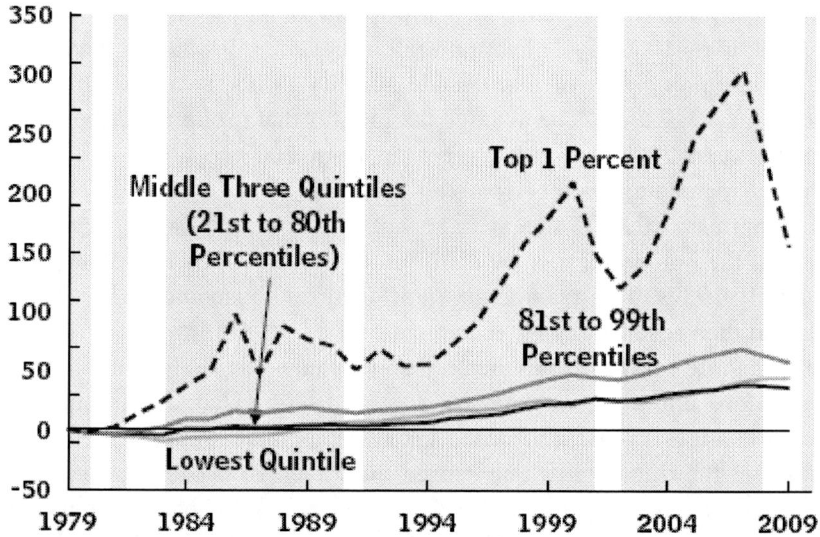

Source: Congressional Budget Office.

Notes: After-tax income is the sum of market income and government transfers, minus federal tax liabilities. Market income is composed of labor income, business income, capital gains, capital income (excluding capital gains), income received in retirement for past services, and other sources of income. Government transfers are cash payments and in-kind benefits from social insurance and other government assistance programs. For more detailed definitions of income, see the appendix.

Quintiles, or fifths, are created by ranking households by their before-tax income. Quintiles contain equal numbers of people.

Federal taxes include individual and corporate income taxes, social insurance (or payroll) taxes, and excise taxes.

Figure 6. Cumulative Growth in Average After-Tax Income Adjusted for Inflation, by Income Group, 1979 to 2009; (Percentage of 1979 income).

2010 AND BEYOND

Although the detailed data that form the basis of CBO's estimates in this report are available only through 2009, other data can provide some insight into changes in the distribution of income and federal taxes in 2010 and 2011. Those data suggest that overall income continued to grow slowly in 2010 and 2011 and that income for households toward the higher end of the distribution increased more rapidly than income for households elsewhere in the income distribution in 2010. Average federal tax rates probably remained near their post-1979 low levels in both 2010 and 2011.

The Bureau of Economic Analysis (BEA) estimates that real per capita personal income grew by 1.1 percent in 2010 and 1.8 percent in 2011.[6] Personal income excluding transfer payments grew a little more slowly than personal income including transfer payments in 2010 and a little more rapidly in 2011.

In contrast, data from the Current Population Survey (CPS) have led the Census Bureau to estimate that real mean household income fell 2.3 percent between 2009 and 2010. In the CPS data, the decline in income was greater for households at the bottom of the income distribution than for those at the middle and the top.

Tabulations by the Internal Revenue Service of individual income tax returns filed for 2010 tell another, slightly different, story. Real income per return rose more than 2 percent from 2009 to 2010—a gain that exceeds the change in income in either the BEA or CPS data— perhaps because income from capital gains, which is excluded from those other measures of income, rose rapidly.[7] Income went up more rapidly for higher-income taxpayers than for other taxpayers—by more than 10 percent for those filing returns with income in the top 1 percent of the distribution of all returns. The share of total before-tax income reported on those tax returns rose by 1.5 percentage points, with capital gains accounting for much but not all of that gain. That increase reversed about one-third of the 2007–2009 decline in the share of income reported to the IRS on returns with income in the top 1 percent of all returns.

Total federal tax revenue grew slowly in 2010 and 2011. Receipts in fiscal year 2010 were 15.1 percent of gross domestic product (GDP), matching 2009 as the lowest share of GDP since 1950. They rebounded slightly in fiscal year 2011, to 15.4 percent of GDP. Those figures imply that average federal tax rates probably did not rise much in 2010 or 2011.

DIFFERENCES WITH EARLIER ESTIMATES

This report makes two significant changes to the methodology that CBO previously used in estimating average federal tax rates. The agency has changed:

- Its allocation of the incidence of the federal corporate income tax, and
- Its method for valuing government-provided health insurance.

Those changes alter CBO's estimates somewhat: The change in the assumed incidence of the corporate income tax makes the federal tax system appear a bit less progressive, and the change in valuing government-provided health insurance increases the measured level and growth of income for many households with low income. However, those methodological changes do not alter this report's basic findings about the distribution of income and federal taxes.

CBO has also changed the way in which it adjusts for inflation. The agency now uses the personal consumption expenditures (PCE) price index, also referred to as the PCE deflator, rather than the consumer price index. The PCE price index generally shows slightly less inflation than does the consumer price index, making measured growth in real income larger for all income groups.

Incidence of the Corporate Income Tax

In previous reports, CBO allocated the entire economic burden of the corporate income tax to owners of capital in proportion to their capital income. CBO has reevaluated the research on that topic, and in this report it allocates 75 percent of the federal corporate income tax to capital income and 25 percent to labor income.

The incidence of the corporate income tax is uncertain. In the very short term, corporate shareholders are likely to bear most of the economic burden of the tax; but over the longer term, as capital markets adjust to bring the after-tax returns on different types of capital in line with each other, some portion of the economic burden of the tax is spread among owners of all types of capital. In addition, because the tax reduces capital investment in the United States, it reduces workers' productivity and wages relative to what they otherwise would be, meaning that at least some portion of the economic burden of the tax over the longer term falls on workers. That reduction in investment probably occurs in part through a reduction in U.S. saving and in part through decisions to invest more savings outside the United States (relative to what would occur in the absence of the U.S. corporate income tax); the larger the decline in saving or outflow of capital, the larger the share of the burden of the corporate income tax that is borne by workers.

CBO recently reviewed several studies that use so-called general-equilibrium models of the economy to determine the long-term incidence of the corporate income tax. The results of those studies are sensitive to assumptions about the values of several key parameters, such as the ease with which capital can move between countries. Using assumptions that reflect the central tendency of published estimates of the key parameters yields an estimate that about 60 percent of the corporate income tax is borne by owners of capital and 40 percent is borne by workers.[8]

However, standard general-equilibrium models exclude important features of the corporate income tax system that tend to increase the share of the corporate tax borne by corporate shareholders or by capital owners in general.[9] For example, standard models generally assume that corporate profits represent the "normal" return on capital (that is, the return that could be obtained from making a risk-free investment). In fact, corporate profits partly represent returns on capital in excess of the normal return, for several reasons: Some corporations possess unique assets such as patents or trademarks; some choose riskier investments that have the potential to provide above-normal returns; and some produce goods or services that face little competition and thereby earn some degree of monopoly profits. Some estimates indicate that less than half of the corporate tax is a tax on the normal return on capital and that the remainder is a tax on such excess returns.[10] Taxes on excess returns are probably borne by the owners of the capital that produced those excess returns. Standard models also generally fail to incorporate tax policies that affect corporate finances, such as the preferences afforded to corporate debt under the corporate income tax. Increases in the corporate tax will increase the subsidy afforded to domestic debt, increasing the relative return on debt-financed investment in the United States and drawing new investment from overseas, thus reducing the net amount of capital that flows out of the country. In addition, standard models generally do not account for corporate income taxes in other countries; those taxes also reduce the amount of capital that flows out of this country because of the U.S. corporate income tax.

Those factors imply that workers bear less of the burden of the corporate income tax than is estimated using standard general-equilibrium models, but quantifying the magnitude of the impact of the factors is difficult. CBO chose to allocate 25 percent of the burden of the corporate income tax to workers and assigned that amount to households in proportion to their labor income. CBO allocated the remaining 75 percent to owners of capital and assigned that tax to households in proportion to their income from interest, dividends, adjusted capital gains, and rents.[11] (The agency used capital gains scaled to their long-term historical level given the size of the economy and the tax rate that applies to them—called "adjusted capital gains"—rather than actual capital gains so as to smooth out large year-to-year variations in the total amount of gains realized.)

Because the share of labor income received by higher-income households is smaller than the share of capital income received by those households, CBO's revision to the allocation of the federal corporate income tax shifts more of that tax to households who are lower in the income distribution. For 2009, the change in methodology reduced the share of the corporate tax paid by households in the top percentile of before-tax income by 12 percentage points. The estimated share of the corporate tax in that year paid by the rest of the top quintile rose by 3 percentage points, and the estimated shares paid by the lowest quintile through the fourth quintile rose by 1, 2, 3, and 4 percentage points, respectively.

The change in the allocation of the corporate tax has a larger impact on the average tax rate for households in the top percentile than for households in other income groups. For 2009, that change lowered the average tax rate by 1.0 percentage point for the top percentile and raised it by 0.2 to 0.3 percentage points for the rest of the top quintile and for the other four quintiles (see Table 4). Because CBO includes corporate income tax payments in before-tax income on the basis of the households to which those corporate taxes are assigned (increasing each household's income by the amount of corporate income tax that the household is estimated to pay), changing the allocation of the corporate tax affects that measure of income. For 2009, that change raised average before-tax income by less than $50 for the lowest quintile, by roughly $100 for the second and middle quintiles, and by $300 for the fourth quintile. In contrast, the change lowered average before-tax income for the highest percentile by more than $14,000.

Valuation of Government-Provided Health Insurance

Health insurance provided though Medicare, Medicaid, and the Children's Health Insurance Program (CHIP) represents a significant and growing portion of government transfers. CBO assigned a higher value to that insurance for the estimates in this report than in previous analyses of the distribution of household income and federal taxes.

Receiving health insurance enhances the economic wellbeing of recipients, enabling them to obtain health care services at a reduced out-of-pocket cost and thereby to consume more health care without giving up other forms of consumption. Accordingly, CBO includes estimated values of health insurance—whether provided by an employer or the government—in its analyses of household income. However, assigning a value to health insurance is difficult because it is unclear how much households would be willing to pay for that insurance.[12]

Some recipients of health insurance might prefer to receive a cash payment equal to the employer's or government's cost of that insurance because then they could choose whether to use all of that cash payment to purchase insurance on their own or to use some or all of it for other purposes. Therefore, the value of the health insurance to some recipients is lower than the cost of providing it, particularly for some low-income recipients, whose consumption of other goods and services is tightly constrained by their lack of resources. For other recipients, though, the value of health insurance is higher than the cost of providing it, because in many cases the bundle of services provided through insurance cannot be purchased by an individual household at a price equal to the employer's or government's cost. Determining how much the value of the insurance to recipients differs from the cost of providing it is impossible without knowing the preferences of individual recipients.

Analyses of the distribution of income differ greatly in their treatment of health insurance. The Census Bureau's primary definition of household income excludes the value of health insurance, as do most studies based on income tax returns, whereas the Census Bureau's alternative definitions of income reflect the so-called fungible value of Medicare, Medicaid, and CHIP.[13] That fungible value is designed to represent the amount of resources freed up for other uses by the government-provided health insurance, up to the average cost to the government of providing that insurance.

Table 4. Effects of Changes in Methodology on Estimates of the Distribution of Income and Average Federal Tax Rates, 2009

Before-Tax Income Group	Previous Methodology	Current Methodology (New incidence of corporate income tax and new valuation of government-provided health insurance)	Change from New Incidence of Corporate Income Tax	Change from New Valuation of Government-Provided Health Insurance
		Average Before-Tax Income (2009 dollars)[a]		
Lowest Quintile	18,900	23,500	*	4,600
Second Quintile	41,700	43,400	100	1,600
Middle Quintile	63,600	64,300	100	600
Fourth Quintile	93,100	93,800	300	400
Highest Quintile	223,800	223,500	-500	200
All Quintiles	86,600	88,400	0	1,800
81st to 90th Percentiles	131,100	131,700	400	200
91st to 95th Percentiles	175,200	175,800	500	100
96th to 99th Percentiles	271,500	271,800	*	300
Top 1 Percent	1,234,600	1,219,700	-14,500	-400
		Average Federal Tax Rate		
		(Rates in percent; changes in percentage points)		
Lowest Quintile	-0.2	1.0	0.2	1.0
Second Quintile	6.8	6.8	0.3	-0.3
Middle Quintile	11.4	11.1	0.2	-0.5
Fourth Quintile	15.1	15.1	0.2	-0.2
Highest Quintile	23.4	23.2	-0.1	-0.1
All Quintiles	17.7	17.4	0	-0.3
81st to 90th Percentiles	18.6	18.8	0.3	-0.1
91st to 95th Percentiles	20.9	21.1	0.2	**
96th to 99th Percentiles	24.1	24.1	0.1	-0.1
Top 1 Percent	29.9	28.9	-1.0	**

Source: Congressional Budget Office.

Notes: CBO has revised its allocation of the incidence of the corporate income tax and its method for valuing government-provided health insurance. In this analysis, CBO has allocated 75 percent of corporate income taxes to capital owners and 25 percent to workers. Also, CBO has valued government-provided health insurance at the average cost to the government (total cost to the government divided by the number of program participants) of providing that insurance, as estimated by the Census Bureau. Those revisions are discussed in more detail in the report.

Before-tax income is the sum of market income and government transfers. Market income is composed of labor income, business income, capital gains, capital income (excluding capital gains), income received in retirement for past services, and other sources of income. Government transfers are cash payments and in-kind benefits from social insurance and other government assistance programs. For more detailed definitions of income, see the appendix.

Quintiles, or fifths, are created by ranking households by their before-tax income. Quintiles contain equal numbers of people. Federal taxes include individual and corporate income taxes, social insurance (or payroll) taxes, and excise taxes.

* = between -$50 and $50; ** = between -0.05 percentage points and 0.05 percentage points.

a. Income amounts have been rounded to the nearest $100.

Specifically, for each household, the Census Bureau compares the household's income with an estimate of the cost to the household of meeting its basic needs for food and housing. If a household does not have enough income to meet those basic needs, the Census Bureau assumes that the household would spend nothing on health care in the absence of the government programs, and it sets the fungible value of health insurance for that household equal to zero. For households with some income above what is necessary to meet their basic needs, the fungible value is set equal to the amount of income above that basic standard, up to the average cost to the government of providing that insurance. One study used both the fungible value of health insurance from the CPS and measures of medical spending constructed from the Medical Expenditure Panel Survey (MEPS).[14] Another study replaced the CPS measures of health insurance with its own estimates of the government's average cost of providing that insurance, again derived from the MEPS.[15]

In previous reports, CBO included in before-tax income the so-called fungible value of Medicare, Medicaid, and CHIP as defined and estimated by the Census Bureau using data from the CPS. In this report, CBO instead included in household income the full value of Medicare, Medicaid, and CHIP, defined to equal the Census Bureau's estimate of the average cost to the government of providing that insurance. CBO's new treatment of government-provided health insurance is consistent with CBO's long-standing treatment of employers' contributions to health insurance, for which the full cost is included in before-tax income.[16]

The change in the valuation of health insurance provided through Medicare, Medicaid, and CHIP has a significant effect on measured income, especially for households near the bottom of the income distribution. The aggregate difference between the Census Bureau's fungible values and the government's average costs was roughly $200 billion for 2009. The change in valuation adds that amount to the before-tax income of households whose other before-tax income does not exceed the cost of meeting its basic needs for food and housing by more than the government's average cost of providing that insurance. The change in methodology increased CBO's estimate of average income for households in the bottom quintile of the before-tax income distribution by roughly $4,600 (or nearly 25 percent) and for households in the second quintile by roughly $1,600 (see Table 4 on page 19).

The average federal tax rate for the population as a whole is 0.3 percentage points lower because of the increase in measured household income. Although one might expect the change to lower average tax rates the most for households in the lowest income quintile, the change actually boosts the average tax rate for that group by a percentage point. That increase occurs because the higher valuation of government-provided health insurance causes about one-eighth of the households in the bottom quintile under CBO's earlier methodology (roughly 3 million households) to be classified in the second quintile under CBO's new methodology, and it causes a corresponding number of households to be classified in the bottom quintile rather than the second quintile. The households who moved out of the bottom quintile generally had much lower cash income than did those who moved into it: The average household in the bottom quintile under both methodologies had about $10,000 in cash wages, compared with $3,000 for the average household who moved out of the bottom quintile and $21,000 for the average household who moved into that quintile. Because households who moved into the bottom quintile had more income from taxable sources, their average tax rates were more than 5 percentage points higher, on average, than those of the households they replaced; as a result, the average tax rate for households in the lowest quintile rose. That reranking of households more than offset the decline in the average tax rate caused by the additional income for the bottom quintile.

The change in valuation also increases the measured longterm growth of income, especially for households near the bottom of the income distribution. The government's average cost of providing Medicare, Medicaid, and CHIP has risen more rapidly than has household income from most other sources, and including that full cost in income leads to faster growth of measured income for households receiving those benefits.[17]

Supplemental tables, available on CBO's Web site, show estimated household income and average federal tax rates using a measure of income that includes only the fungible value of Medicare, Medicaid, and CHIP.

Measuring Inflation

In this report, CBO adjusted household income for the effects of inflation using the personal consumption expenditures price index. That index is constructed by the Bureau of Economic Analysis as part of the national income and product accounts. Previously, CBO had used the Bureau of Labor Statistics' research series of the consumer price index for all urban consumers (CPI-U-RS). The average annual inflation rate over the 1979–2009 period was about 0.2 percentage points lower as measured by the PCE price index than as measured by the CPI-U-RS. In CBO's judgment, the PCE price index is a more appropriate deflator for the measures of income used in this report because its scope includes health care services purchased by third parties on behalf of people (services that are included in the measures of income used in this report) and because it more fully accounts for the adjustments that consumers make to their spending patterns as some prices change relative to other prices.[18]

APPENDIX: METHODOLOGY

In estimating the distribution of household income and federal taxes, the Congressional Budget Office (CBO) draws on various data sources and makes judgments about the best way to use those data. This appendix explains the methodology CBO used in this report.

Sources of Data

Information on household income for this analysis comes from two primary sources: the Statistics of Income (SOI), collected by the Internal Revenue Service, and the Current Population Survey (CPS), collected by the Census Bureau. The core data come from the SOI, a nationally representative sample of individual income tax returns that has increased in size from roughly 90,000 returns around 1980 to more than 300,000 returns in recent years. CBO used the full Individual Income Tax file, which contains more detail than the public-use version of the file. CBO supplemented those SOI data with data from the Annual Social and Economic Supplement to the CPS; those survey data contain information on the demographic characteristics and income of a large sample of households.

Both the SOI and the CPS lack important information needed for estimating and comparing after-tax household income over time. The SOI lacks information about couples and individuals who do not file a federal tax return; in addition, it does not report all income from government cash transfer programs, has no information on the receipt of in-kind transfers and benefits, and is organized by tax-filing units rather than households. The CPS lacks detailed information on high-income households, does not report capital gains, underreports other income from capital, and lacks information on the deductions and adjustments necessary to compute taxes.

To overcome the limitations of both data sources, CBO statistically matched each SOI record to a corresponding CPS record on the basis of demographic characteristics and income. Each pairing resulted in a new record that took on the demographic characteristics of the CPS record and the income reported in the SOI. (Some types of income, such as certain transfers and in-kind benefits, appear only in the CPS; values for those items were drawn directly from that survey.) Because not all households have to file tax returns, some households do not appear in the SOI. Therefore, after all SOI records were matched to CPS records, the remaining CPS records were recorded as households who did not file an income tax return, and their income values were taken directly from the CPS. CBO then estimated the tax liability for each record.

Who Pays Taxes?

In its analysis, CBO assumed that households bear the economic cost of the taxes they pay directly, such as individual income taxes and the employee's share of payroll taxes. CBO further assumed—as do most economists— that employers pass on their share of payroll taxes to employees by paying lower wages than they would otherwise pay. Therefore, CBO included the employer's share of payroll taxes in households' before-tax income and in households' taxes.

CBO also assumed that the economic cost of excise taxes falls on households according to their consumption of taxed goods (such as tobacco and alcohol). Excise taxes on intermediate goods, which are paid by businesses, were attributed to households in proportion to their overall consumption. CBO assumed that each household spent the same amount on taxed goods as a similar household with comparable income is reported to spend in the Bureau of Labor Statistics' Consumer Expenditure Survey.

Far less consensus exists about how to allocate corporate income taxes (and taxes on capital income generally). In this analysis, CBO allocated 75 percent of the burden of corporate income taxes to owners of capital in proportion to their income from interest, dividends, adjusted capital gains, and rents. The agency used capital gains scaled to their long-term historical level given the size of the economy and the tax rate that applies to them rather than actual capital gains so as to smooth out large year-to-year variations in the total amount of gains realized. CBO allocated 25 percent of the burden of corporate income taxes to workers in proportion to their labor income.

Measuring Income

This analysis uses three measures of household income: market income; market income plus government transfers (referred to as before-tax income); and market income plus government transfers, minus federal tax liabilities (referred to as after-tax income).

Market income includes the following components:

- *Labor income*—Cash wages and salaries, including those allocated by employees to 401(k) plans; employer-paid health insurance premiums; the employer's share of Social Security, Medicare, and federal unemployment insurance payroll taxes; and the share of corporate income taxes borne by workers.
- *Business income*—Net income from businesses and farms operated solely by their owners, partnership income, and income from S corporations.
- *Capital gains*—Profits realized from the sale of assets. Increases in the value of assets that have not been realized through sales are not included in market income.
- *Capital income (excluding capital gains)*—Taxable and tax-exempt interest, dividends paid by corporations (but not dividends from S corporations, which are considered part of business income), positive rental income, and the share of corporate income taxes borne by owners of capital.
- *Other income*—Income received in retirement for past services and other sources of income.

Government transfers consist of cash payments from Social Security, unemployment insurance, Supplemental Security Income, Temporary Assistance for Needy Families (and its predecessor, Aid to Families with Dependent Children), veterans' programs, workers' compensation, and state and local government assistance programs. They also include the value of in-kind benefits, such as Supplemental Nutrition Assistance Program vouchers (formerly known as food stamps), school lunches and breakfasts, housing assistance, energy assistance, and benefits provided by Medicare, Medicaid, and the Children's Health Insurance Program. (The value of health insurance is measured on the basis of the Census Bureau's estimates of the average cost to the government of providing such insurance.)

After-tax income is the sum of market income and government transfers, minus federal tax liabilities. In assessments of the impact of various taxes, individual income taxes are allocated directly to households paying those taxes. Social insurance, or payroll, taxes are allocated to households paying those taxes directly or paying them indirectly through their employers. Corporate income taxes are allocated to households according to their share of capital and labor income, as described above. Federal excise taxes are allocated to households according to their consumption of the taxed good or service.

Adjusting Income for Differences among Households

CBO used households as the unit of analysis for this report. A household consists of the people who share a housing unit, regardless of their relationships. The presumption is that households make joint economic decisions, although that may not be true in every case (in a group house, for example). Households may comprise more than one taxpaying unit, such as a married couple and their adult children living together.

Households with identical income may differ in ways that bear on their economic status. Importantly, a larger household needs more income to support a given standard of living than does a smaller household. However, economies of scale in some types of consumption—housing, in particular—mean that two people generally do not need twice the income to live as well as an individual living alone. Therefore, to rank households by their standard of living, it is probably appropriate to divide household income by an adjustment factor that is between one (which would result only in household income and would not capture the greater needs of larger households) and the number of people in the household (which would produce household income per capita and would not capture the benefits of shared consumption). CBO chose to adjust for household size by dividing household income by the square root of the number of people in the household, counting adults and children equally.[1] Households were then ranked by their adjusted income and grouped into quintiles that contain equal numbers of people. Because household sizes vary, different quintiles generally contain slightly different numbers of households.

Adjusting the income of households for other differences in their circumstances that affect their standard of living might also be desirable. For example, the prices of goods and services vary among locations, and households can incur different costs associated with working, such as the costs of commuting and child care expenses, depending on how many members of the household are employed. In this analysis, however, CBO did not attempt to adjust for those additional differences.

Types of Households

Supplemental tables, available on CBO's Web site, show household income and average federal tax rates for three types of households: those with members under age 18 (households with children), those headed by a person age 65 or older and with no member under age 18 (elderly childless households), and all others (nonelderly childless households). The tables group households into quintiles by position in the income distribution across the full population, not by distribution within each type of household, so each type of household need not be evenly spread across the income quintiles.

End Note for Summary

[1] For information on definitions of income, the allocation of taxes, and the ranking of households, see "Notes and Definitions" at the front of this report.

End Notes

[1] See Congressional Budget Office, *Trends in the Distribution of Household Income Between 1979 and 2007* (October 2011), and *Average Federal Taxes by Income Group* (June 2010). The methodology used in this report differs somewhat from that used in the earlier studies, although the primary conclusions of the earlier studies are unaffected by the changes in

methodology. In conjunction with this report, CBO has also published supplemental tables that present estimates for the 1979–2009 period derived using the current methodology. Those tables are available at www.cbo.gov/ publication/43310.

[2] Real personal income—the measure of income the Bureau of Economic Analysis (BEA) uses in the national income and product accounts (NIPAs)—also declined from 2007 to 2009, though not by nearly as much as CBO's income measure. Much of that difference in the two measures occurs because CBO includes capital gains in market income; in contrast, BEA does not include capital gains as part of personal income in the NIPAs.

[3] In the federal budget, the refundable portion of income tax credits is counted as outlays. In fiscal year 2009, the revenues collected from individual income taxes (which do not count the refundable portion of those tax credits) were a slightly larger share of gross domestic product (6.6 percent) than the revenues collected from social insurance taxes (6.4 percent).

[4] The Internal Revenue Service made those payments to taxpayers in 2008 on the basis of information provided on their 2007 tax returns. Taxpayers who did not receive an advance payment could take a credit against their 2008 tax liabilities. In this analysis, CBO counted such payments as part of 2008 tax liabilities.

[5] This report includes only federal taxes. CBO did not include state and local taxes in this analysis because of the difficulty of estimating them for individual households.

[6] BEA's measures of income are different from those used by CBO. Personal income, as defined by BEA, is the income that people receive in return for their provision of labor, land, and capital used in current production plus net current transfer payments they receive from business and government.

[7] Income is measured here as income from taxable sources plus tax-exempt interest and some nontaxable Social Security benefits. That is the broadest measure reported on tax returns, but it omits several nontaxable sources of income that are included in CBO's measure of before-tax income, such as employer-sponsored health benefits and payments from the Supplemental Nutrition Assistance Program.

[8] Jennifer Gravelle, *Corporate Tax Incidence: Review of General Equilibrium Estimates and Analysis*, Congressional Budget Office Working Paper 2010-03 (May 2010).

[9] For a detailed discussion of many of these features, see Alan Auerbach, "Who Bears the Corporate Tax? A Review of What We Know," in James M. Poterba, ed., *Tax Policy and the Economy*, vol. 20 (MIT Press, 2006).

[10] William M. Gentry and R. Glenn Hubbard, "Distributional Implications of Introducing a Broad-Based Consumption Tax," in James M. Poterba, ed., *Tax Policy and the Economy*, vol. 11 (MIT Press, 1997); Eric Toder and Kim Rueben, "Should We Eliminate Taxation of Capital Income?," in Henry J. Aaron, Leonard E. Burman, and C. Eugene Steurle, eds., *Taxing Capital Income* (Urban Institute, 2007); and Julie-Anne Cronin and others, *Distributing the Corporate Income Tax: Revised U.S. Treasury Methodology,* Office of Tax Analysis Technical Paper 5 (Department of Treasury, Office of Tax Analysis, May 2012).

[11] Although shareholders of corporations would bear the portion of the corporate tax that is a tax on excess returns, measures of that share of the corporate tax are imprecise, as are efforts to identify corporate shareholders in the available data. CBO did not try to differentiate among capital owners in assigning the portion of the corporate income tax that falls on capital owners.

[12] For a detailed discussion of issues involved in valuing insurance, see Bureau of the Census, *Conference on the Measurement of Noncash Benefits*, vol. 1, *Proceedings* (1986), www.census.gov/ hhes/www/poverty/publications/measurementconf.pdf.

[13] Arthur F. Jones Jr. and Daniel H. Weinberg, *The Changing Shape of the Nation's Income Distribution, 1974–1998,* Current Population Reports, Series P60-204 (Census Bureau, June 2000); Michael Strudler and others, *Analysis of the Distribution of Income, Taxes, and Payroll Taxes via Cross Section and Panel Data, 1979– 2004* (Internal Revenue Service, Statistics of Income Division, 2006); and Thomas Piketty and Emmanuel Saez, "Income Inequality in the United States, 1913–1998," *Quarterly Journal of Economics*, vol. 118, no. 1 (February 2003), pp. 1–39.

[14] See Gary Burtless and Pavel Svaton, "Health Care, Health Insurance, and the Distribution of American Incomes," *Forum for Health Economics & Policy*, vol. 13, no. 1 (2010), www.bepress.com/fhep/13/1/1.

[15] See Richard V. Burkhauser and Kosali I. Simon, *Measuring the Impact of Health Insurance on Levels and Trends in Inequality*, Working Paper 15811 (National Bureau of Economic Research, March 2010).

[16] The Census Bureau assigns the average cost of government-provided health insurance to beneficiaries on the basis of average expenditures by state and by risk class. It estimates the cost of employers' contributions to health insurance on the basis of a separate survey of employers. A full description of the methods used to value noncash benefits is provided in Bureau of the Census, *Measuring the Effect of Benefits and Taxes on Income and Poverty: 1992*, Current Population Reports, Series P60, No. 186RD (September 1993), pp. viii–ix and B-1 to B-5.

[17] See Congressional Budget Office, *Trends in the Distribution of Household Income Between 1979 and 2007* (October 2011), Appendix C.

[18] For a more detailed discussion of alternative measures of inflation, see Congressional Budget Office, *Using a Different Measure of Inflation for Indexing Federal Programs and the Tax Code* (February 2010).

End Note for Appendix

[1] That adjustment implies that each additional person increases a household's needs but does so at a decreasing rate. For example, a household consisting of a married couple with two children and income of $80,000 would have an adjusted income of $40,000 ($80,000 divided by the sqaure root of 4) and would have the equivalent economic ranking of a single person with income of $40,000 or a married couple without children with income of about $56,600 ($56,600 divided by the square root of 2 is approximately $40,000). See Constance F. Citro and Robert T. Michael, eds., *Measuring Poverty: A New Approach* (National Academy Press, 1995).

In: Distribution of Household Income … ISBN: 978-1-63117-264-9
Editor: Travis Honeyfield

Chapter 2

THE DISTRIBUTION OF HOUSEHOLD INCOME AND FEDERAL TAXES, 2010*

Edward Harris

NOTES AND DEFINITIONS

Numbers in the text, tables, and figures may not add up to totals because of rounding.

Unless otherwise indicated, all years referred to in this study are calendar years. Federal fiscal years run from October 1 to September 30.

Some of the figures have white vertical bars that indicate the duration of recessions. (A recession extends from the peak of a business cycle to its trough.)

Market income consists of labor income, business income, capital gains (profits realized from the sale of assets), capital income (excluding capital gains), income received in retirement for past services, and other sources of income.

Before-tax income is the sum of market income and government transfers.

After-tax income is the sum of market income and government transfers, minus federal tax liabilities.

---

* Edward Harris wrote this report which was released by the Congressional Budget Office, December 2013.

Government transfers include cash payments and in-kind benefits from social insurance and other government assistance programs.

Federal tax liabilities are the amount a household owes on the basis of income received in a year, regardless of when taxes are paid. Individual income taxes are allocated directly to the households that pay those taxes. Social insurance, or payroll, taxes are allocated to the households that pay those taxes either directly or indirectly through employers. Excise taxes are allocated to households according to their consumption of the taxed goods or services. Corporate income taxes are allocated to households according to their shares of capital and labor income. Specifically, 75 percent of corporate income taxes is allocated to owners of capital in proportion to their income from interest, dividends, adjusted capital gains, and rents. (Capital gains are scaled to a long-term historical amount, given the size of the economy and the applicable tax rate, so as to smooth out large year-to-year variations in the total amount of gains realized.) The remaining 25 percent of corporate income taxes is allocated to workers in proportion to their labor income.

Average federal tax rates are calculated by dividing federal tax liabilities by before-tax income. When refundable tax credits, such as the earned income tax credit and the child tax credit, exceed the other federal tax liabilities of the households in an income group, those households are said to have a negative average tax rate. (Refundable tax credits are not limited to the amount of income tax owed before the credits are applied.)

Income groups are defined by ranking all people by income, adjusted for household size—that is, divided by the square root of the number of people in a household, which consists of the people who share a housing unit, regardless of relationship. Quintiles, or fifths, contain equal numbers of people, as do percentiles, or hundredths. If a household has negative income (that is, if its business or investment losses are larger than its other income), it is excluded from the lowest income category but included in totals.

Income is adjusted for inflation using the personal consumption expenditure price index, which is calculated by the Bureau of Economic Analysis.

SUMMARY

The increase in the nation's economic activity in 2010 affected households' income, federal tax liabilities, and federal tax rates. In this report, the Congressional Budget Office (CBO) presents its estimates of the distribution of household income and federal taxes in 2010, and it compares those estimates with estimates for the preceding three decades. The report also discusses the effects of changes in tax rules on the distribution of federal taxes in 2013.

How Were Federal Taxes Distributed in 2010?

The average federal tax rate for all households in 2010— that is, tax liabilities divided by income (including government transfer payments) before taxes—was 18.1 percent. To examine the effect of taxes on households with different amounts of income, CBO divided the nation's households into five groups of equal size, arrayed by before-tax income. In 2010, the federal tax rate for the bottom quintile of the income distribution was 1.5 percent and that for the top quintile was 24.0 percent (see Figure 1). The top 1 percent of all households in the United States had an average federal tax rate of 29.4 percent in 2010.[1]

Higher-income households pay much more in federal taxes than do their lower-income counterparts: They have a much greater share of the nation's before-tax income, and they pay a much larger proportion of that income in taxes. Households in the top quintile (including the top percentile) paid 68.8 percent of all federal taxes, households in the middle quintile paid 9.1 percent, and those in the bottom quintile paid 0.4 percent of federal taxes.

How Did Federal Taxes Affect the Distribution of Income in 2010?

Federal taxes caused the distribution of after-tax income in 2010 to be slightly more even among quintiles than was the distribution of before-tax income. Households in the bottom four quintiles received shares of after-tax income that were about 1 percentage point greater than their shares of before-tax income. For example, households in the bottom quintile received 5.1 percent of before-tax income and 6.2 percent of after-tax income, and those in the middle quintile received 14.2 percent of before-tax income and 15.4 percent of after-tax income. In contrast, households in the highest quintile received 51.9 percent of before-tax income and 48.1 percent of after-tax income.

How Did the Distribution of Income and Federal Taxes Change From 2009 to 2010?

Average before-tax income rose by 2.7 percent from 2009 to 2010 in real (inflation-adjusted) terms, but the increase was uneven. Income rose by about 1 percent for households in the lowest quintile and by less than 1 percent for households in each of the three middle quintiles (see Figure 2). In contrast, income grew by about 5 percent for households in the top quintile and by about 16 percent for households in the top percentile. Those increases recouped some of the steep declines that occurred from 2007 to 2009 for the highest-income taxpayers, although it left their incomes well below the prerecession peaks. As a result of the uneven growth from 2009 to 2010, the share of income for the top 1 percent increased by 1.6 percentage points, and the share for the middle three quintiles taken together fell by 1.3 percentage points.

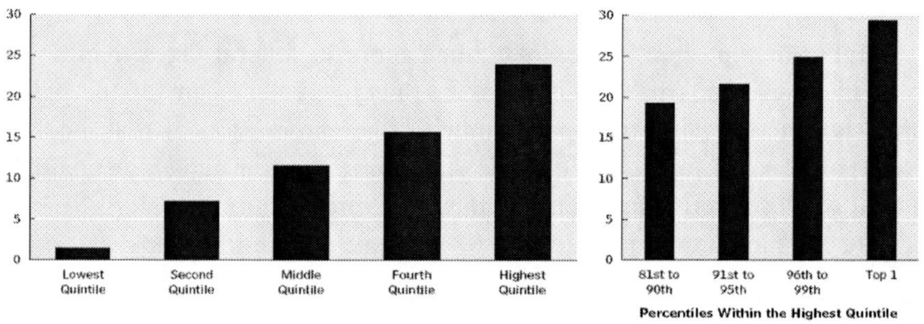

Source: Congressional Budget Office.

Notes: Average federal tax rates are calculated by dividing federal tax liabilities by before-tax income.

Before-tax income is the sum of market income and government transfers. Market income is composed of labor income, business income, capital gains, capital income (excluding capital gains), income received in retirement for past services, and other sources of income. Government transfers are cash payments and in-kind benefits from social insurance and other government assistance programs.

Federal taxes include individual and corporate income taxes, social insurance (or payroll) taxes, and excise taxes.

Income groups are created by ranking households by before-tax income. Quintiles (fifths) contain equal numbers of people; percentiles (hundredths) contain equal numbers of people as well.

For more detailed definitions of income, see Appendix A.

Figure 1. Average Federal Tax Rates, by Income Group, 2010; (Percent).

The average federal tax rate for all households rose by 0.8 percentage points from 2009 to 2010. The increases were fairly even across income groups, with each quintile seeing an increase of between 0.4 and 0.8 percentage points. Average individual and corporate income tax rates rose and the average payroll tax rate fell, driven largely by changes in the composition of the tax base rather than by changes in tax provisions.

What Are the Longer-Term Trends in the Distribution of Federal Taxes?

Even with the increases in average federal tax rates in 2010, the average rate for each income group was below the rate that prevailed for that group in the 1990s and most of the 2000s (see Figure 3). For most income groups, average federal tax rates in 2010 were near the lowest rates for the 1979–2010 period. The exception was households in the top 1 percent, whose average federal tax rate in 2010 was significantly above its low in the mid-1980s.

How Will Changes in Tax Rules Between 2010 and 2013 Affect Average Federal Tax Rates?

Current federal tax rules differ from those of 2010 in important ways:

- Several provisions affecting high-income taxpayers, originally enacted in the Economic Growth and Tax Relief Reconciliation Act of 2001 (EGTRRA) and the Jobs and Growth Tax Relief Reconciliation Act of 2003 (JGTRRA), were allowed to expire in 2013.
- The Making Work Pay tax credit expired at the end of 2010, and payroll tax rates that had been reduced in 2011 and 2012 were reset in 2013 to their earlier amounts.
- New taxes for high-income taxpayers, enacted with the Affordable Care Act, took effect in 2013.[2]

For this report, CBO estimated average federal tax rates for 2013 by simulating tax liabilities under 2013 tax rules using reported 2010 incomes and making an adjustment for estimated aggregate income growth between 2010 and 2013. That analytical approach was taken to isolate the effects of changes in tax rules and does not account for shifts in the distribution of income that might have occurred between 2010 and 2013. Tax rates will increase overall as a result of the changes in tax rules, with the largest increases at either end of the income distribution:

Average rates are projected to rise by 1.6 percentage points for households in the lowest quintile, by 1.0 percentage point for those in the middle quintile, and by 4.2 percentage points for the top percentile. For most income groups, average tax rates under 2013 law are projected to remain below those in 2007, the year before the recession began, and well below those for most of the past three decades. For the top 1 percent of households, however, average rates under 2013 law will be higher than in any year since 1997.

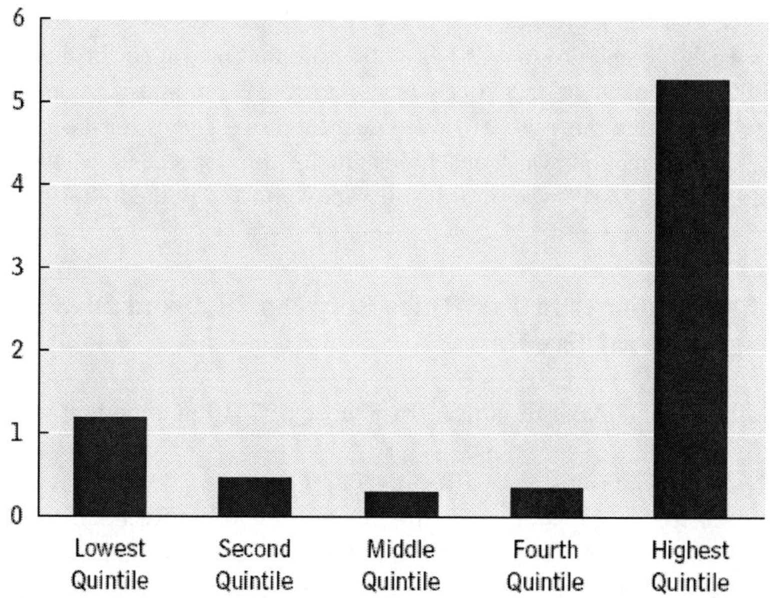

Source: Congressional Budget Office.

Notes: Before-tax income is the sum of market income and government transfers. Market income is composed of labor income, business income, capital gains, capital income (excluding capital gains), income received in retirement for past services, and other sources of income. Government transfers are cash payments and in-kind benefits from social insurance and other government assistance programs.

Income groups are created by ranking households by before-tax income. Quintiles (fifths) contain equal numbers of people.

For more detailed definitions of income, see Appendix A.

Figure 2. Change in Before-Tax Income, by Income Group, 2009 to 2010; (Percent).

DATA AND METHODS

In this report, CBO examines the distribution of household income and federal tax rates, focusing on data from calendar year 2010. The current analysis builds on earlier work that covered the period from 1979 through 2009.[3]

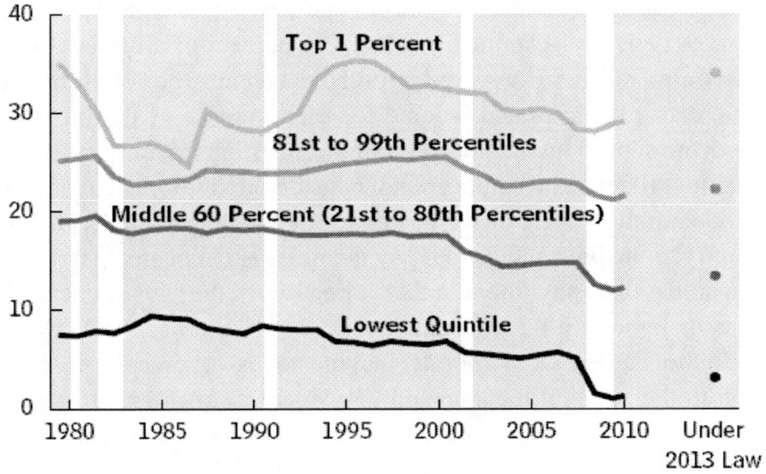

Source: Congressional Budget Office.

Notes: CBO estimated average tax rates under 2013 law by simulating tax liabilities under 2013 tax rules using reported 2010 incomes and making adjustments for aggregate income growth between 2010 and 2013.

Average federal tax rates are calculated by dividing federal tax liabilities by before-tax income.

Before-tax income is the sum of market income and government transfers. Market income is composed of labor income, business income, capital gains, capital income (excluding capital gains), income received in retirement for past services, and other sources of income. Government transfers are cash payments and in-kind benefits from social insurance and other government assistance programs.

Federal taxes include individual and corporate income taxes, social insurance (or payroll) taxes, and excise taxes.

Income groups are created by ranking households by before-tax income. Quintiles (fifths) contain equal numbers of people; percentiles (hundredths) contain equal numbers of people as well.

For more detailed definitions of income, see Appendix A.

Figure 3. Average Federal Tax Rates, by Income Group, 1979 to 2010 and Under 2013 Law; (Percent).

CBO used data on tax returns from the Internal Revenue Service and survey data collected by the Census Bureau to estimate income—including government transfer payments—and federal taxes for a representative sample of households in each year from 1979 through 2010. (Appendix A gives more information on the data and on CBO's methodology.) This report shows average federal tax rates for various income categories for the four largest sources of federal revenue—individual income taxes, payroll taxes, corporate income taxes, and excise taxes— and for the four types combined. Together, those sources typically account for at least 95 percent of all federal revenues. This report also discusses average household income (both before and after taxes) and shares of taxes and income for each quintile of the income distribution and for subgroups of the top quintile. Customs duties, estate and gift taxes, and miscellaneous receipts are not considered in the current analysis.[4]

In modeling the effects of various taxes, CBO allocated individual income taxes directly to the households that pay them. It also allocated payroll taxes to the households that pay them either directly to the government through deductions or indirectly through employers' contributions. CBO allocated 75 percent of the burden of corporate income taxes to owners of capital, in proportion to their capital income, and 25 percent to workers, in proportion to their labor income. Excise taxes are allocated to households according to their consumption of the taxed goods or services.

This study uses several measures of income. Market income consists of labor income, business income, capital gains, capital income (excluding capital gains), income received in retirement for past services, and other sources of income. (Labor income includes the value of income received in-kind from sources such as employer-paid health insurance premiums.) Before-tax income is the sum of market income and government transfers, and after-tax income is before-tax income minus federal tax liabilities.

The unit of analysis for this report is the household, which is considered to consist of the people who share a housing unit, regardless of their relationship to one another. To construct income groups, CBO ranked households by income with an adjustment for household size to account for the differing needs of households of various sizes. Larger households, for example, need more income than smaller ones to achieve the same standard of living, but they generally do not need proportionally more income. CBO adjusted for household size by dividing household income by the square root of the number of people in the household, counting adults and children equally.

This study focuses on annual income, showing average income in different years for different households grouped by income. Annual income is only one measure of economic well-being, however, and this analysis does not assess trends in the distribution of other measures, such as household income measured over longer periods, household consumption, or household wealth.[5] Because household income varies over time, a household in a given segment of the income distribution in one year could be in a different segment in another year.

ESTIMATES FOR 2010

Between 2009 and 2010, real before-tax income grew by 2.7 percent across all households. That increase was uneven, however, with income rising by 16.0 percent for households in the top income percentile but by less than 1 percent for households in the bottom four quintiles. The share of income accruing to households in the top 1 percent rose, but it fell for most other income groups. Average tax rates rose for all income quintiles (and the top percentile) by less than 1 percentage point, primarily because individual and corporate income taxes increased. Increases in after-tax income were smaller than increases in before-tax income because of the rise in average tax rates.

Households' Before-Tax Income

Before-tax income, the sum of market income and government transfers, is distributed very unevenly because of the very uneven distribution of market income, which is partially equalized through government transfers (see Box 1). In 2010, households in the lowest quintile received 5.1 percent of all before-tax income, or about $24,100 per household (see Table 1 on page 8). Those in the middle fifth received 14.2 percent, or $65,400 per household. Households in the top quintile received 51.9 percent, or about $239,100 per household.

Real average before-tax income grew by 2.7 percent from 2009 to 2010 across all households, but that growth was not uniform across the income distribution. Households in the bottom income quintile in 2010 had income that was 1.2 percentage points higher than those in the same group in 2009 (the households in the various groups in 2010, however, were not necessarily the same as those a year before). Households in the middle three income quintiles, and in the 81st through 90th percentiles, in 2010 had income that was less than a percentage point higher than in 2009. Income grew by 1.8 percent for households in the 91st through 95th percentiles, by 3.5 percent for households in the 96th through 99th percentiles, and by 16.0 percent for households in the top 1 percent of the income distribution. That increase for taxpayers with the highest income recouped some of the steep declines that occurred from 2007 to 2009, although among the top 1 percent, income remained well below its prerecession peak. As a result of the uneven growth, the share of before-tax income received by the top 1 percent grew from 13.3 percent to 14.9 percent, and the share received by all income groups below the 96th percentile fell.

That uneven pattern reflects substantially different growth rates for various sources of income as the economy began to recover from the recession, with little change in the distribution of each type. Several income sources that accrue predominantly to higher-income households declined steeply from 2007 to 2009 but then rebounded somewhat in 2010. For example, real capital gains income rose by 55 percent from 2009 to 2010, although it was still 60 percent below the peak reached in 2007, and dividends and business income also grew rapidly from 2009 to 2010, by 10 percent and 12 percent, respectively. In contrast, wage income, the most important source for households in the lower 80 percent of the distribution, grew by less than 1 percent in real terms from 2009 to 2010. Transfer income, which is quite important to the lower income quintiles, grew by less than 2 percent in real terms.

Average Federal Tax Rates

Average tax rates depend both on tax laws and on economic conditions. The overall average federal tax rate (federal tax liabilities divided by before-tax household income) was 18.1 percent in 2010 (see Table 2 on page 9). And of that overall rate, the rates for individual income taxes and payroll taxes were 7.7 percent of household income each, the corporate income tax rate was 2.1 percent, and the excise tax rate was 0.6 percent.

Although the average individual income tax rate historically has been higher than the payroll tax rate, in 2010 the two were equal. Two factors explain that unusual circumstance. First, nonwage income (such as interest, dividends, and capital gains) declined much more than wage income did in the recent recession. Despite a partial recovery in 2010, nonwage income was still low, thus reducing income taxes but not payroll taxes. Second, the American Recovery and Reinvestment Act of 2009 (ARRA) introduced new refundable income tax credits and expanded some existing credits, which reduced individual income taxes in 2009 and 2010. In its analysis, CBO measured individual income taxes net of refundable credits.[6] In 2011, some components of ARRA expired, and a reduction in the payroll tax rate took effect, so average income tax rates probably rose in that year while average payroll tax rates declined.

Box 1. The Distribution of Market Income, Transfers, and Federal Taxes

This report examines the distribution of taxes among households ranked by before-tax income, a broad measure that includes market income and government transfers. Another method of examining those distributions would involve ranking households on the basis of market income—labor, business, capital, and retirement income—and then examining how transfers and federal taxes are distributed among the various groups of households. Market income is very unevenly distributed. In 2010, households in the lowest income quintile (the bottom one-fifth of all households ranked by market income) received 2.3 percent of that income, or about $8,100 per household (see the table), on average. Households in the middle quintile received 13.0 percent, or an average of about $54,800; those in the top quintile received 57.9 percent, or an average of about $234,400.

Government transfers increase income in all groups, but those increases, both in dollars and as a percentage of market income, are larger for groups with lower market income. Social Security and Medicare are the two largest transfer programs. Combined benefits from those programs averaged $8,900 for all households in 2010, and other transfers averaged $4,100.[1] Social Security and Medicare go predominantly to elderly households, many of which have low market income. Households in the lowest quintile received 36.2 percent of the total benefits from Social Security and Medicare (averaging $14,200 per household), households in the middle quintile received 16.7 percent of those benefits, and those in the highest quintile received 11.4 percent.[2] Other transfers—including unemployment benefits, payments from the Supplemental Nutrition Assistance Program, and benefits from Medicaid and the Children's Health Insurance Program—go even more disproportionately to households in the lower portion of the market income distribution.

Households in the bottom quintile received 47.0 percent of benefits from other transfers (averaging $8,500 per household), households in the middle quintile received 13.3 percent of those benefits, and those in the highest quintile received 6.2 percent.

Because the federal tax system is progressive—average rates rise with income—shares of taxes paid exceed shares of income for the highest income group, and the opposite holds true for the bottom four quintiles. (For this analysis, the Congressional Budget Office considered refundable tax credits as negative income taxes rather than transfers.) Shares of taxes paid are comparable whether households are ranked by before-tax income or market income.

Because of taxes and transfers, the after-tax income distribution is a little more equal than the market income distribution. In 2010, households in the highest income quintile received 57.9 percent of market income and 47.2 percent of after-tax income. In that year, households in the fourth quintile received a somewhat lower share of after-tax income than market income, and households in the bottom three quintiles received larger shares of after-tax income than market income—with the largest difference for households in the lowest quintile, which received 2.3 percent of market income and 9.3 percent of after-tax income.

[1] The values of most transfers are based on amounts reported in the Current Population Survey. However, the values of transfers from Medicare, Medicaid, and the Children's Health Insurance Program are based on the average cost to the government of providing those benefits. See Appendix A for more details.

[2] The Congressional Budget Office recently undertook a more comprehensive analysis of federal spending in 2006. That study adjusted transfers as reported in the Current Population Survey to equal budgetary totals as reported in the Monthly Treasury Statements issued by the Treasury Department. Although the study's methodology was similar to that used for this report, it differed in some important respects, most notably by arraying only nonelderly households into income quintiles. For more details, see Congressional Budget Office, The Distribution of Federal Spending and Taxes in 2006 (November 2013), www.cbo.gov/ publication/44698.

Distribution of Market Income, Transfers, and Federal Taxes, by Market Income Group, 2010

		Government Transfers			
Market Income Group	Market Income	Social Security and Medicare	Other Transfers	Federal Taxes	After-Tax Income
	Average Amount (Dollars)[a]				
Lowest Quintile	8,100	14,200	8,500	*	30,800
Second Quintile	30,700	10,300	4,900	2,500	43,400
Middle Quintile	54,800	7,900	2,900	8,100	57,400
Fourth Quintile	87,700	5,500	1,900	16,100	78,900
Highest Quintile	234,400	5,200	1,300	58,900	181,900
All Quintiles	79,300	8,900	4,100	16,600	75,500
	Share (Percent)				
Lowest Quintile	2.3	36.2	47.0	**	9.3
Second Quintile	7.4	22.1	22.8	2.8	11.0
Middle Quintile	13.0	16.7	13.3	9.2	14.3
Fourth Quintile	21.0	11.7	8.8	18.4	19.8
Highest Quintile	57.9	11.4	6.2	69.3	47.2
All Quintiles	100.0	100.0	100.0	100.0	100.0

Source: Congressional Budget Office.

Notes: Market income is composed of labor income, business income, capital gains, capital income (excluding capital gains), income received in retirement for past services, and other sources of income. Government transfers are cash payments and in-kind benefits from social insurance and other government assistance programs. Federal taxes include individual and corporate income taxes, social insurance (or payroll) taxes, and excise taxes. After-tax income is the sum of market income and government transfers, minus federal tax liabilities.

Income groups are created by ranking households by before-tax income. Quintiles (fifths) contain equal numbers of people. For more detailed definitions of income, see Appendix A.

* = between zero and $50; ** = between zero and 0.05 percent.

a. Income amounts have been rounded to the nearest $100.

The overall average federal tax rate rose from 17.3 percent of income in 2009 to 18.1 percent in 2010. The average corporate income tax rate (corporate taxes divided by before-tax household income) rose by 0.6 percentage points, and the average individual income tax rate rose by 0.5 percentage points. Those increases were partially offset by a 0.3 percentage-point decline in the average payroll tax rate. The average excise tax rate was unchanged. Those rate changes were attributable primarily to changes in the income subject to the various taxes; tax rules changed little from 2009 to 2010.

Several factors contributed to the increase in the individual income tax rate:

- Income from taxable sources (especially capital gains, dividends, and business income) rose more than did income from nontaxable sources (such as transfer payments, employer contributions to health insurance, and tax-exempt interest);
- Growth in itemized deductions was outstripped by growth in income;
- The distribution of taxable income shifted upward, so more income was taxed in higher tax brackets; and
- Tax credits grew more slowly than income did, in large part because many credits have fixed dollar caps.

The average corporate income tax rate (again, defined for this analysis as corporate taxes divided by before-tax household income) rose from 1.5 percent in 2009 to 2.1 percent in 2010. Corporate tax liabilities rose by 43 percent, from $153 billion to $219 billion. That change reflects a rapid increase in the profits of C corporations—the measure of income subject to the corporate income tax.

Aggregate payroll tax rates (household payroll tax liabilities divided by before-tax household income) fell because wages and salaries—the measure subject to the payroll tax—rose more slowly than did other types of income, pushing down payroll taxes as a share of total income. Also, earnings for high earners rose by more than earnings for lower earners, so roughly 1 percent more of household earnings was above the maximum subject to Social Security payroll taxes ($106,800 in 2010), pushing down the average tax rate. In 2010, 84.2 percent of earnings was below that cap and therefore subject to the Social Security tax, a historically low percentage. (In 1983, the first year under the existing system for setting the taxable maximum, 90 percent of earnings fell below the cap. Since then, that percentage has generally fallen, reaching a low of about 83 percent, first in 2000 and again in 2007.)

Table 1. Distribution of Before- and After-Tax Income, by Income Group, 2009 and 2010

Income Group	Average Income (2010 Dollars)[a]			Share of Income (Percent)		
	2009	2010	Change (Percent)	2009	2010	Change (Percentage points)
	Before-Tax Income					
Lowest Quintile	23,800	24,100	1.2	5.1	5.1	*
Second Quintile	44,000	44,200	0.5	9.8	9.6	-0.2
Middle Quintile	65,200	65,400	0.3	14.6	14.2	-0.4
Fourth Quintile	95,100	95,500	0.4	21.1	20.4	-0.7
Highest Quintile	227,100	239,100	5.3	50.8	51.9	1.1
All Quintiles	89,800	92,200	2.7	100.0	100.0	n.a.
81st to 90th Percentiles	134,000	134,600	0.5	14.9	14.6	-0.3
91st to 95th Percentiles	178,400	181,600	1.8	10.1	9.9	-0.2
96th to 99th Percentiles	276,700	286,400	3.5	12.5	12.5	*
Top 1 Percent	1,237,300	1,434,900	16.0	13.3	14.9	1.6
	After-Tax Income					
Lowest Quintile	23,600	23,700	0.7	6.1	6.2	0.1
Second Quintile	41,000	41,000	0	11.1	10.9	-0.2
Middle Quintile	58,000	57,900	-0.1	15.7	15.4	-0.3
Fourth Quintile	80,800	80,600	-0.3	21.6	21.0	-0.6
Highest Quintile	174,500	181,800	4.2	47.2	48.1	0.9
All Quintiles	74,200	75,500	1.8	100.0	100.0	n.a.
81st to 90th Percentiles	109,000	108,700	-0.3	14.7	14.3	-0.4
91st to 95th Percentiles	140,700	142,400	1.2	9.6	9.5	-0.1
96th to 99th Percentiles	209,900	215,200	2.6	11.4	11.5	0.1
Top 1 Percent	879,800	1,013,100	15.1	11.5	12.8	1.3

Source: Congressional Budget Office.

Notes: Average federal tax rates are calculated by dividing federal tax liabilities by before-tax income.

Before-tax income is the sum of market income and government transfers. Market income is composed of labor income, business income, capital gains, capital income (excluding capital gains), income received in retirement for past services, and other sources of income. Government transfers are cash payments and in-kind benefits from social insurance and other government assistance programs.

After-tax income is the sum of market income and government transfers, minus federal tax liabilities.

Federal taxes include individual and corporate income taxes, social insurance (or payroll) taxes, and excise taxes.

Income groups are created by ranking households by before-tax income. Quintiles (fifths) contain equal numbers of people; percentiles (hundredths) contain equal numbers of people as well.

For more detailed definitions of income, see Appendix A.

* = between -0.05 and 0.05 percentage points; n.a. = not applicable. a. Income amounts have been rounded to the nearest $100.

Table 2. Average Federal Tax Rates, by Income Group, 2009 and 2010 (Percentage of before-tax income)

Income Group	All Federal Taxes	Individual Income Taxes	Social Insurance Taxes	Corporate Income Taxes	Excise Taxes
			2010		
Lowest Quintile	1.5	-9.2	8.4	0.7	1.6
Second Quintile	7.2	-2.3	7.8	0.7	1.0
Middle Quintile	11.5	1.6	8.3	0.8	0.8
Fourth Quintile	15.6	5.0	9.0	1.0	0.6
Highest Quintile	24.0	13.8	6.7	3.1	0.4
All Quintiles	18.1	7.7	7.7	2.1	0.6
81st to 90th Percentiles	19.3	8.1	9.4	1.2	0.5
91st to 95th Percentiles	21.6	10.7	8.9	1.5	0.4
96th to 99th Percentiles	24.9	15.1	7.1	2.3	0.4
Top 1 Percent	29.4	20.1	2.2	6.9	0.2
			2009		
Lowest Quintile	1.0	-9.3	8.3	0.5	1.5
Second Quintile	6.7	-2.6	7.9	0.5	0.9
Middle Quintile	11.1	1.3	8.4	0.6	0.8
Fourth Quintile	15.0	4.6	9.1	0.7	0.6
Highest Quintile	23.2	13.4	7.1	2.2	0.4
All Quintiles	17.3	7.2	8.0	1.5	0.6
81st to 90th Percentiles	18.7	7.7	9.6	0.9	0.5
91st to 95th Percentiles	21.1	10.3	9.3	1.1	0.5

Income Group	All Federal Taxes	Individual Income Taxes	Social Insurance Taxes	Corporate Income Taxes	Excise Taxes
96th to 99th Percentiles	24.2	14.6	7.5	1.7	0.4
Top 1 Percent	28.9	21.0	2.5	5.2	0.2
			Change		
Lowest Quintile	0.5	0.1	0.1	0.2	0.1
Second Quintile	0.5	0.3	-0.1	0.2	0.1
Middle Quintile	0.4	0.3	-0.1	0.2	*
Fourth Quintile	0.6	0.4	-0.1	0.3	*
Highest Quintile	0.8	0.4	-0.4	0.9	*
			Change		
All Quintiles	0.8	0.5	-0.3	0.6	*
81st to 90th Percentiles	0.6	0.4	-0.2	0.3	*
91st to 95th Percentiles	0.5	0.4	-0.4	0.4	-0.1
96th to 99th Percentiles	0.7	0.5	-0.4	0.6	*
Top 1 Percent	0.5	-0.9	-0.3	1.7	*

Source: Congressional Budget Office.

Notes: Average federal tax rates are calculated by dividing federal tax liabilities by before-tax income.

Before-tax income is the sum of market income and government transfers. Market income is composed of labor income, business income, capital gains, capital income (excluding capital gains), income received in retirement for past services, and other sources of income. Government transfers are cash payments and in-kind benefits from social insurance and other government assistance programs.

Federal taxes include individual and corporate income taxes, social insurance (or payroll) taxes, and excise taxes.

Income groups are created by ranking households by before-tax income. Quintiles (fifths) contain equal numbers of people; percentiles (hundredths) contain equal numbers of people as well.

For more detailed definitions of income, see Appendix A.

* = between -0.05 and 0.05 percent.

Distribution of Federal Taxes Across the Income Scale

The federal tax system is progressive—that is, average tax rates generally rise with income. In 2010, households in the bottom quintile of the before-tax income distribution paid 1.5 percent of their before-tax income in federal taxes, households in the middle quintile paid 11.5 percent, and households in the top quintile paid 24.0 percent (see Figure 4 and see Table 2 on page 9). Average rates rose within the top quintile, and households in the top 1 percent of the before-tax income distribution faced an average rate of 29.4 percent.

From 2009 to 2010, the average federal tax rate for all households rose by 0.8 percentage points. That increase was fairly even across income groups. Each of the bottom four income quintiles had increases of between 0.4 and 0.6 percentage points, and the highest income quintile had only a slightly larger increase of 0.8 percentage points.

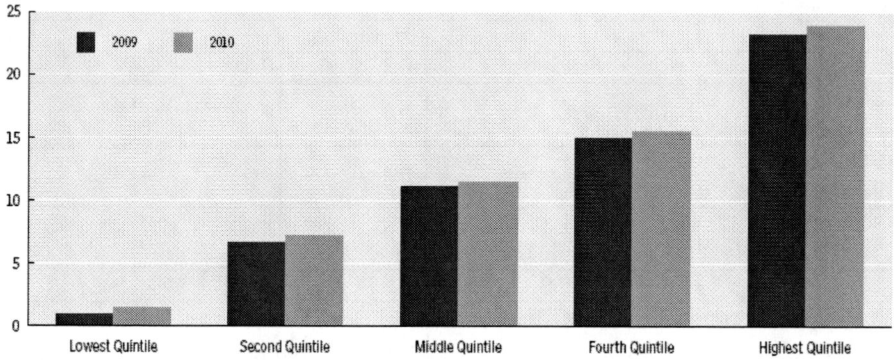

Source: Congressional Budget Office.

Notes: Average federal tax rates are calculated by dividing federal tax liabilities by before-tax income.

Before-tax income is the sum of market income and government transfers. Market income is composed of labor income, business income, capital gains, capital income (excluding capital gains), income received in retirement for past services, and other sources of income. Government transfers are cash payments and in-kind benefits from social insurance and other government assistance programs.

Federal taxes include individual and corporate income taxes, social insurance (or payroll) taxes, and excise taxes.

Income groups are created by ranking households by before-tax income. Quintiles (fifths) contain equal numbers of people.

For more detailed definitions of income, see Appendix A.

Figure 4. Average Federal Tax Rates, by Income Group, 2009 and 2010; (Percent).

Because average tax rates rise with income, the share of taxes paid by higher-income households exceeded their share of before-tax income, and the opposite was true for lower-income households. In 2010, households in the highest quintile received 51.9 percent of before-tax income and paid 68.8 percent of federal taxes; households in the top 1 percent received 14.9 percent of before-tax income and paid 24.2 percent of federal taxes (see Figure 5 and see Table 2 on page 9).

In all other quintiles, the share of federal taxes was smaller than the share of before-tax income: Households in the bottom quintile received 5.1 percent of income and paid 0.4 percent of taxes, and households in the middle quintile received 14.2 percent of income and paid 9.1 percent of taxes.

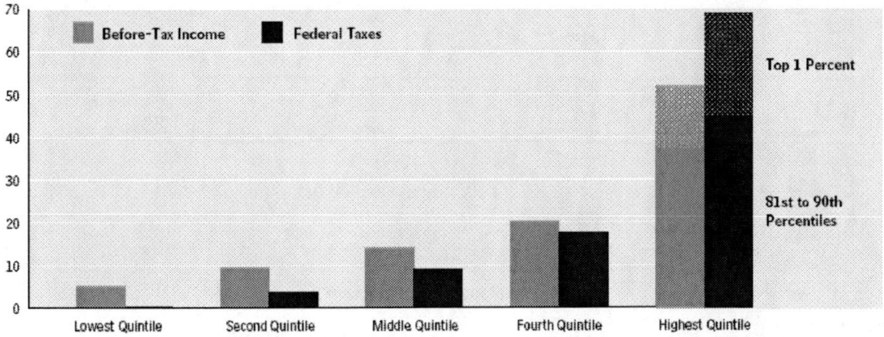

Source: Congressional Budget Office.

Notes: Average federal tax rates are calculated by dividing federal tax liabilities by before-tax income.

Before-tax income is the sum of market income and government transfers. Market income is composed of labor income, business income, capital gains, capital income (excluding capital gains), income received in retirement for past services, and other sources of income. Government transfers are cash payments and in-kind benefits from social insurance and other government assistance programs.

Federal taxes include individual and corporate income taxes, social insurance (or payroll) taxes, and excise taxes.

Income groups are created by ranking households by before-tax income. Quintiles (fifths) contain equal numbers of people; percentiles (hundredths) contain equal numbers of people as well.

For more detailed definitions of income, see Appendix A.

Figure 5. Shares of Before-Tax Income and Federal Taxes, by Income Group, 2010; (Percent).

Individual Income Taxes

Much of the progressivity of the federal tax system derives from the individual income tax. In 2010, the lowest quintile's average rate for the individual income tax was -9.2 percent and the second income quintile's rate was -2.3 percent (see Figure 6 and see Table 2 on page 9). (A group can have a negative income tax rate if its refundable tax credits exceed the income tax otherwise owed.) The average income tax rate was 1.6 percent for the middle quintile, 5.0 percent for the fourth quintile, and 13.8 percent for the top quintile. The top 1 percent of the population, on average, paid 20.1 percent of their income in individual income taxes.

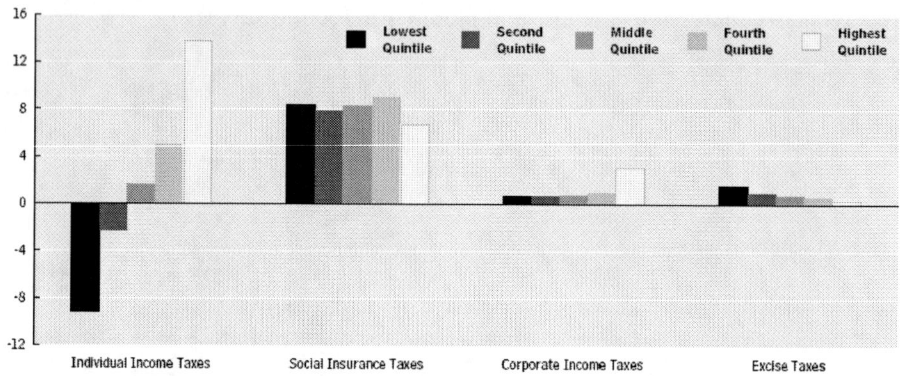

Source: Congressional Budget Office.

Notes: Average federal tax rates are calculated by dividing federal tax liabilities by before-tax income.

Before-tax income is the sum of market income and government transfers. Market income is composed of labor income, business income, capital gains, capital income (excluding capital gains), income received in retirement for past services, and other sources of income. Government transfers are cash payments and in-kind benefits from social insurance and other government assistance programs.

Federal taxes include individual and corporate income taxes, social insurance (or payroll) taxes, and excise taxes.

Income groups are created by ranking households by before-tax income. Quintiles (fifths) contain equal numbers of people. For more detailed definitions of income, see Appendix A.

Figure 6. Average Federal Tax Rates, by Income Group and Tax Source, 2010; (Percent).

Within each income group, there is considerable variation in average tax rates, attributable to several factors, including the composition of income, family structure, tax preferences, and the progressive rate structure. (Appendix B discusses those variations in more detail.) For example, although the lowest quintile's average rate for the individual income tax was about -9 percent, more than one-quarter of the households in that quintile had an average rate that was below -15 percent, more than one-quarter had a rate of zero or higher, and nearly half had an average rate that was between -15 percent and zero.

Variation in income tax rates declines among higher-income groups. For example, in the fourth income quintile, for which the average rate for the individual income tax was 5 percent, the rate for about one-quarter of the households was below 3 percent, and the rate for about one-quarter was 7 percent or higher.

From 2009 to 2010, the individual income tax rate rose slightly for all income groups other than the top 1 percent. Rates rose by 0.1 percentage point for households in the lowest quintile, they rose by 0.3 percentage points in the second and middle quintiles, and they rose by 0.4 percentage points in the fourth and highest income quintiles. The reasons for the increases are varied. In the bottom quintiles, income and income taxes increased somewhat, but tax credits were flat, so the average tax rate was higher. In the fourth quintile and the bottom portion of the top quintile, itemized deductions grew more slowly than income, pushing the average rate up. The average income tax rate fell for the top 1 percent of the income distribution, however, by 0.9 percentage points. That drop was primarily the result of large increases in capital gains and dividend income, which are taxed at lower rates than other forms of income. Despite that drop in the average rate, the share of income taxes paid by the top 1 percent rose by 0.3 percentage points because of the rapid increase in income among people in that group (see Table 3). Specifically, the increase in their income more than offset the decline in their tax rate, boosting their share of taxes.

Social Insurance Taxes

Average rates for payroll taxes are fairly flat across most of the income distribution but lower at the top. In 2010, the average payroll tax rate was 8.4 percent for the lowest quintile, 7.8 percent for the second quintile, 8.3 percent for the middle quintile, and 9.0 percent for the fourth quintile (see Table 2 on page 9). The highest quintile's rate was 6.7 percent, and households in the top percentile faced a rate of 2.2 percent. The rate for higher-income households is lower than that for others in part because more of those households' earnings are above the maximum subject to Social Security payroll taxes and in part because earnings are a smaller share of their total income. Payroll taxes account for the largest share of taxes paid by households in all but the top quintile.

Between 2009 and 2010, the average payroll tax rate (measured as a percentage of before-tax income) fell from 8.0 percent to 7.7 percent. The change was not uniform across the income distribution, however. On average, rates rose by 0.1 percentage point for the lowest quintile, fell by 0.1 percentage point for the middle three quin-tiles, and fell by 0.4 percentage points for the highest quintile. Those changes largely reflect a changing composition of income for the various groups—wages and salaries as a share of income increased for households in the bottom quintile but declined for all other groups, more so for higher-income households. The increase in earnings at the bottom reflects a changing composition of that group: The income of low-income workers rose by less than did the income of low-income nonworkers, and thus more workers fell into the lowest income quintile.

Table 3. Shares of Federal Taxes, by Income Group, 2009 and 2010 (Percent)

Income Group	All Federal Taxes	Individual Income Taxes	Social Insurance Taxes	Corporate Income Taxes	Excise Taxes
			2010		
Lowest Quintile	0.4	-6.2	5.6	1.7	13.4
Second Quintile	3.8	-2.9	9.8	3.1	15.4
Middle Quintile	9.1	2.9	15.4	5.5	18.7
Fourth Quintile	17.6	13.3	23.9	9.5	20.6
Highest Quintile	68.8	92.9	45.1	78.8	31.5
All Quintiles	100.0	100.0	100.0	100.0	100.0
81st to 90th Percentiles	15.5	15.4	17.8	8.4	12.0
91st to 95th Percentiles	11.9	13.8	11.5	7.1	7.1
96th to 99th Percentiles	17.2	24.6	11.5	13.7	7.5
Top 1 Percent	24.2	39.0	4.2	49.5	4.9
			2009		
Lowest Quintile	0.3	-6.6	5.3	1.8	12.2
Second Quintile	3.8	-3.5	9.6	3.2	15.2
Middle Quintile	9.4	2.7	15.4	5.8	18.9
Fourth Quintile	18.3	13.4	24.0	10.1	21.3
Highest Quintile	68.0	94.1	45.4	77.2	31.9
All Quintiles	100.0	100.0	100.0	100.0	100.0
81st to 90th Percentiles	16.0	15.9	17.8	8.7	12.5
91st to 95th Percentiles	12.3	14.4	11.7	7.3	7.5
96th to 99th Percentiles	17.4	25.2	11.7	14.0	7.6
Top 1 Percent	22.2	38.7	4.2	47.1	4.4

Income Group	All Federal Taxes	Individual Income Taxes	Social Insurance Taxes	Corporate Income Taxes	Excise Taxes
			Change		
Lowest Quintile	0.1	0.4	0.3	-0.1	1.2
Second Quintile	*	0.6	0.2	-0.1	0.2
Middle Quintile	-0.3	0.2	*	-0.3	-0.2
Fourth Quintile	-0.7	-0.1	-0.1	-0.6	-0.7
Highest Quintile	0.8	-1.2	-0.3	1.6	-0.4
81st to 90th Percentiles	-0.5	-0.5	*	-0.3	-0.5
91st to 95th Percentiles	-0.4	-0.6	-0.2	-0.2	-0.4
96th to 99th Percentiles	-0.2	-0.6	-0.2	-0.3	-0.1
Top 1 Percent	2.0	0.3	*	2.4	0.5

Source: Congressional Budget Office.

Notes: Income groups are created by ranking households by before-tax income. Quintiles (fifths) contain equal numbers of people; percentiles (hundredths) contain equal numbers of people as well.

Before-tax income is the sum of market income and government transfers. Market income is composed of labor income, business income, capital gains, capital income (excluding capital gains), income received in retirement for past services, and other sources of income. Government transfers are cash payments and in-kind benefits from social insurance and other government assistance programs.

Federal taxes include individual and corporate income taxes, social insurance (or payroll) taxes, and excise taxes. For more detailed definitions of income, see Appendix A. * = between -0.05 and 0.05 percent.

The Tax Relief, Unemployment Insurance Reauthorization, and Job Creation Act of 2010 reduced the Social Security payroll tax rate by 2 percentage points in 2011, and two subsequent laws extended that reduction through 2012. That change reduced average payroll tax rates for all income groups for those years. The reduction expired at the end of 2012, and the Social Security tax rate reverted to its original, higher level.

Corporate Income Taxes

The effect of the corporate income tax also increases with income. CBO allocates most of that tax to capital income, which constitutes a larger share of income at the top of the distribution.[7] Households in the highest income quintile paid almost 80 percent of the corporate income tax in 2010. The average rate—corporate taxes as a percentage of before-tax household income—was 3.1 percent for the highest quintile and between 0.7 percent and 1.0 percent for the lowest four income quintiles.

That average tax rate rose across the entire income distribution between 2009 and 2010, reflecting a 43 percent increase in corporate income tax liabilities, which in turn reflected a sharp increase in corporate profits. The tax also became somewhat more skewed to the top of the distribution: The share of the tax paid by the top 1 percent increased from 47.1 percent to 49.5 percent, reflecting a shift in the distribution of capital income, an increasing share of which was earned in the top reaches of the distribution.

Excise Taxes

Excise taxes, most of which are levied on the sale of motor fuels (gasoline and diesel fuel), tobacco products, alcoholic beverages, and aviation-related goods and services (such as aviation fuel and airline tickets), historically have accounted for between 3 percent and 4 percent of all federal taxes. The effect of those taxes, relative to income, is greatest for lower-income households, which tend to spend a larger share of their income on goods and services that are subject to such taxation. Excise tax rates were 1.6 percent for households in the lowest income quintile, 0.8 percent for households in the middle income quintile, and 0.4 percent for households in the highest income quintile. Average rates changed little between 2009 and 2010—by no more than one-tenth of a percentage point for any income group. Shares of excise taxes paid by the groups also changed little.

Households' after-Tax Income

Because average federal tax rates rise with income, the distribution of after-tax income is slightly more even than the distribution of before-tax income.8 In 2010, households in the bottom four quintiles of the before-tax income distribution received a share of after-tax income that was about 1 percentage point larger than their share of before-tax income (see Figure 7 and see Table 1 on page 8). In contrast, households in the highest quintile received 51.9 percent of before-tax income and 48.1 percent of after-tax income.

Increases in after-tax income between 2009 and 2010 were heavily concentrated at the top of the income distribution, largely because of changes in the before-tax income distribution. After-tax income rose by 15.1 percent for the top 1 percent of households and by about 1.9 percent for households in the 91st to 99th percentiles.

Households in the bottom four income quintiles saw changes in their after-tax income that ranged from an increase of 0.7 percent in the lowest quintile to a drop of 0.3 percent in the fourth quintile.

As a consequence, the share of after-tax income accruing to the top percentile of the distribution rose by 1.3 percentage points, and the share earned by most other groups fell.

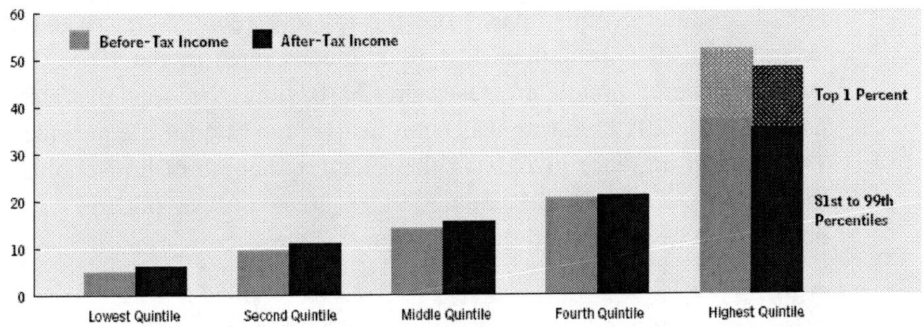

Source: Congressional Budget Office.

Notes: Average federal tax rates are calculated by dividing federal tax liabilities by before-tax income.

Before-tax income is the sum of market income and government transfers. Market income is composed of labor income, business income, capital gains, capital income (excluding capital gains), income received in retirement for past services, and other sources of income. Government transfers are cash payments and in-kind benefits from social insurance and other government assistance programs.

Federal taxes include individual and corporate income taxes, social insurance (or payroll) taxes, and excise taxes. After-tax income is the sum of market income and government transfers, minus federal tax liabilities.

Income groups are created by ranking households by before-tax income. Quintiles (fifths) contain equal numbers of people; percentiles (hundredths) contain equal numbers of people as well.

For more detailed definitions of income, see Appendix A.

Figure 7. Shares of Before- and After-Tax Income, by Income Group, 2010; (Percent).

TRENDS SINCE 1979

Viewed from a longer historical perspective, notable features of the distribution of income and taxes in 2010 include the following:

- The overall average federal tax rate remained near its lowest rate in the 1979–2010 period, despite an increase in 2010.[9] The average rate was lower in 2008, 2009, and 2010 than in all other years in that period, and the 2010 rate of 18.1 percent was well below the period's average rate of 20.9 percent. Although the average individual income tax rate rebounded slightly in 2010 from its low point in 2009, that rate also remained near its low for the period.
- For all income groups apart from the top 1 percent, average federal tax rates in 2010 remained near their lowest rates in the 1979–2010 period, despite small increases in 2010. For the top percentile, however, the 2010 tax rate was near the average rate for the period.
- The marked increase in 2010 in the after-tax income of households in the top 1 percent of the population reversed only a portion of the decline that accompanied the recession.

Average Federal Tax Rates by Source

At 18.1 percent, the 2010 overall average federal tax rate was among the lowest observed in the 1979–2010 period, exceeding only the rates of 2008 and 2009 (see the top panel of Figure 8).

That rate was 22.0 percent in 1979, before declining in the early 1980s and then rising through much of the 1980s and 1990s. It peaked at 22.7 percent in 2000 and then fell sharply after the 2001 recession and the enactment of tax legislation in 2001 and 2003, reaching 19.4 percent in 2003. The rate rebounded somewhat over the next few years, as economic conditions improved, and then dropped sharply in 2008 and 2009 before rising somewhat from 2009 to 2010.

Average rates were lower in 2008, 2009, and 2010 than in all other years in the 1979–2010 period.

The average individual income tax rate peaked at 11.9 percent of household income in 1981 and then declined when the reduction in tax rates enacted in 1981 took effect. Legislation enacted in 1993, along with rapidly rising incomes, pushed the rate up again in the late 1990s; it was 11.7 percent in 2000. The rate fell to 8.3 percent in 2003 as a result of the 2001 and 2003 tax cuts and the recession in 2001. Rates again fell in 2008 and 2009, to a low of 7.2 percent of before-tax household income, largely because of declines in income and changes in tax law. The rate rose somewhat in 2010, mainly because income tax deductions and tax credits grew more slowly than income.

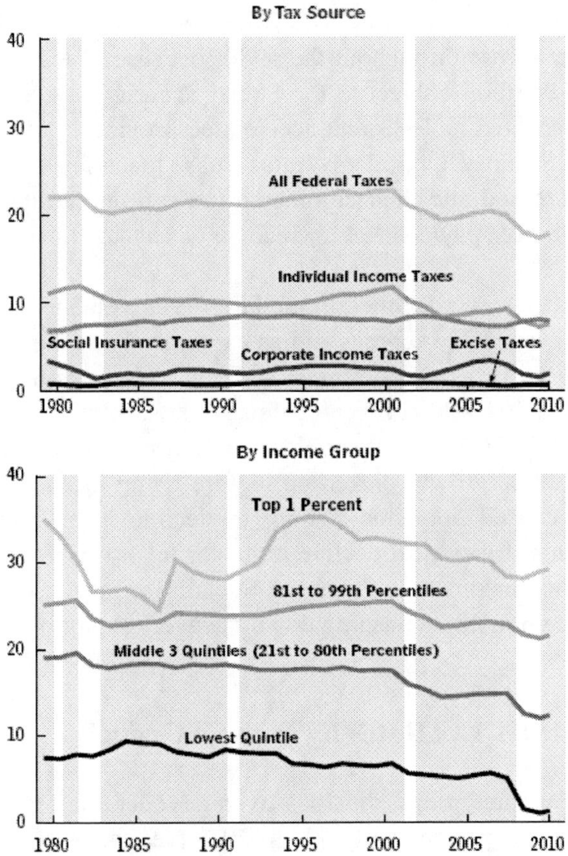

Source: Congressional Budget Office.

Notes: Average federal tax rates are calculated by dividing federal tax liabilities by before-tax income.

Before-tax income is the sum of market income and government transfers. Market income is composed of labor income, business income, capital gains, capital income (excluding capital gains), income received in retirement for past services, and other sources of income. Government transfers are cash payments and in-kind benefits from social insurance and other government assistance programs.

Federal taxes include individual and corporate income taxes, social insurance (or payroll) taxes, and excise taxes.

Income groups are created by ranking households by before-tax income. Quintiles (fifths) contain equal numbers of people; percentiles (hundredths) contain equal numbers of people as well.

For more detailed definitions of income, see Appendix A.

Figure 8. Average Federal Tax Rates, 1979 to 2010; (Percent).

The average payroll tax rate rose from 6.8 percent in 1979 to 7.7 percent in 2010. The rate rose throughout the 1980s because of legislated increases in the maximum earnings subject to the Social Security payroll tax and because of legislation enacted in 1983 that accelerated previously scheduled increases in the Social Security payroll tax rate. Subsequent legislation in the early 1990s first increased and then eliminated the cap on earnings subject to the Hospital Insurance payroll tax (which is used to finance a portion of Medicare).

The payroll tax rate declined in the late 1990s as labor income grew more slowly than other income sources and as earnings above the maximum subject to Social Security taxes grew more rapidly than earnings below that amount. The recession of 2001–2002 reversed those trends, causing the payroll tax rate to rise in the early 2000s. The payroll tax rate resumed its decline in the mid-2000s, as economic growth picked up, before rising in 2008 and 2009, when the recession caused nonlabor income to decline more sharply than labor income and caused wages to decline more for taxpayers with earnings above than below the maximum subject to Social Security taxes. Those trends reversed yet again in 2010, pushing down the average payroll tax rate.

Average Federal Tax Rates by Income Group

For most income groups, the 2009 average federal tax rate was the lowest observed during the period from 1979 to 2010 (see the bottom panel of Figure 8). Those rates increased somewhat for all income groups in 2010, but they remained near their low points. The pattern in the intervening years is more varied, reflecting the interaction of numerous changes to tax law with changes in the composition and distribution of income.

For households in the lowest income group, the average rate fell from 7.5 percent in 1979 to 1.5 percent in 2010. Almost two-thirds of that decline came between 2007 and 2008, largely as a result of ARRA, which created the Making Work Pay tax credit and expanded the earned income tax credit and the child tax credit. The average rate for that group was lower in 2008, 2009, and 2010 than in any other year in the 1979–2010 period. Declines in earlier years were caused mainly by increases in the earned income tax credit, especially in the 1990s. Payroll tax rates rose steadily for households in the lowest income group, offsetting some of the decline in their individual income tax rate.

Households in the middle three income quintiles saw their average tax rates fall by 6.6 percentage points over the period, from 19.1 percent in 1979 to 12.5 percent in 2010. That decline was primarily attributable to a decline in individual income taxes. The average tax rate for the group fell somewhat in the early 1980s and then fluctuated within a fairly narrow range throughout the 1980s and 1990s. Over the 2000–2003 period, the rate declined by 3.1 percentage points, reflecting numerous changes in law enacted in 2001 (notably the expansion of the child tax credit, reductions in tax rates, and increases in the standard deduction for married couples) that lowered taxes for households in the middle quintiles. The average tax rate for those groups rose slightly over the 2003–2007 period before falling by 2.8 percentage points from 2007 to 2009 and then edging up in 2010. The average rate was lower in 2008, 2009, and 2010 than at any other time during the 1979–2010 period.

The average tax rate for households in the 81st to 99th percentiles of the income distribution also reached a low point in 2009—about 4 percentage points below that in 1979—before rising slightly in 2010. That rate fell in the early 1980s and then crept up over the rest of that decade and through the 1990s, so that by 2000 it was slightly above the 1979 rate. The rate fell by 2.9 percentage points between 2000 and 2003, rose modestly from 2003 to 2007, and then fell by another 1.7 percentage points from 2007 to 2009, before rising by 0.7 percentage points in 2010. The average rate was lower in 2008, 2009, and 2010 than at any other time in the 1979–2010 period.

In contrast, in 2010, the average tax rate for households in the top 1 percent of the before-tax income distribution was well above the low point it reached in the early 1980s. The average tax rate for those households fell in the early 1980s and then rose as a result of the enactment of the Tax Reform Act of 1986. The rate for that group then fell somewhat again in the latter half of the 1980s before rising in the 1990s. That climb reflected both the changes in law that boosted tax rates and the group's rapidly increasing income, which caused their average tax rate to rise as more income was taxed in higher tax brackets. The tax rate for households in the top percentile declined after 2000, notably in 2003, when a reduction in the rate for the top tax bracket enacted in 2001 took effect and as further changes in law reduced tax rates on dividends and realized capital gains. The tax rate fell again in 2007, mostly because of declines in corporate income taxes, and then rose somewhat from 2007 to 2009, as sharp declines in capital gains income subjected a larger portion of the income of that group to the tax rates on other income. Their tax rate continued to rise in 2010 because of higher corporate income taxes, muted somewhat by declining rates for the individual income tax. The 2010 tax rate was near the average for the full 1979–2010 period, higher than the rate throughout most of the 1980s, but lower than that in most of the 1990s.

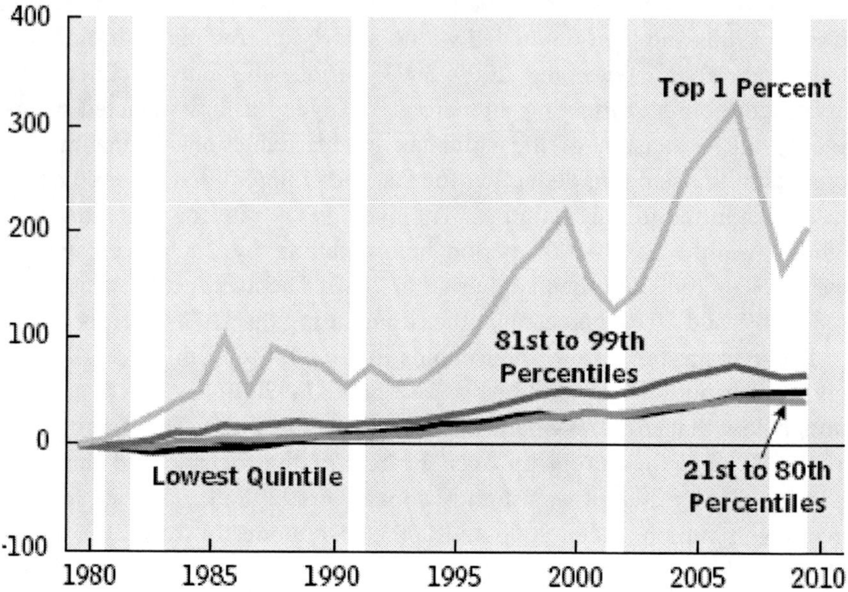

Source: Congressional Budget Office.

Notes: After-tax income is the sum of market income and government transfers, minus federal tax liabilities.

Income groups are created by ranking households by before-tax income. Quintiles (fifths) contain equal numbers of people; percentiles (hundredths) contain equal numbers of people as well.

Before-tax income is the sum of market income and government transfers. Market income is composed of labor income, business income, capital gains, capital income (excluding capital gains), income received in retirement for past services, and other sources of income. Government transfers are cash payments and in-kind benefits from social insurance and other government assistance programs.

Federal taxes include individual and corporate income taxes, social insurance (or payroll) taxes, and excise taxes.

For more detailed definitions of income, see Appendix A.

Figure 9. Cumulative Growth in Average After-Tax Income, by Income Group, 1979 to 2010.

After-Tax Income

For most income groups, after-tax income grew little in 2010. Households in the bottom four income quintiles saw changes in after-tax income that ranged from a 0.7 percent increase for households in the lowest quintile to a 0.3 percent decline for households in the fourth quintile (although the households in a given quintile in 2010 were not necessarily the same as those in that quintile in an earlier year). That change left real after-tax income for the lowest quintile 49 percent higher in 2010 than in 1979 (see Figure 9). Income growth averaged 1.3 percent annually for that group over the period. After-tax income for the middle three quintiles in 2010 was 40 percent higher than in 1979—equivalent to an average annual growth rate of 1.1 percent for the period.

Households in the 81st to 99th percentiles fared somewhat better. Their after-tax income grew by 1.6 percent in 2010, matching the average annual growth rate for the period and raising their after-tax income to 64 percent above its level in 1979.

The top 1 percent of households saw their after-tax income grow by 15 percent from 2009 to 2010, greatly exceeding increases in any other group. That group had seen a steep decline in income between 2007 and 2009, as a result of large declines in capital income, which left the group's income well below its prerecession peak. In 2010, household income for the top 1 percent was 201 percent above the mark for 1979, representing an average annual growth rate of 3.6 percent, far ahead of any other income group.

Developments Since 2010

This report provides estimates of the distribution both of income and of federal taxes through 2010 because the detailed data necessary to estimate distributions for periods after that year were not available when the analysis in this report was undertaken. Many developments since 2010 are likely to have changed those distributions, however, and data that are less detailed than those used in most of this report can provide some insight. Overall income, for example, continued to grow slowly in 2011 and 2012, and CBO expects that income growth will maintain a slow pace in 2013. Tabulations of tax returns and survey data offer mixed signals about changes in the distribution of income in 2011 and 2012; those data are not yet available for 2013. Data on aggregate federal tax revenue suggest that average tax rates probably rose somewhat in 2011 and 2012, but not much above their historically low levels. And tax provisions have changed appreciably since 2010.

CBO estimated average federal tax rates for 2013 by simulating tax liabilities under 2013 tax rules using reported 2010 incomes and making an adjustment for estimated aggregate income growth between 2010 and 2013. That approach suggests that the changes in tax provisions will boost average tax rates for all income groups, with the greatest increases at the top and bottom of the income distribution.

Overall Income Growth

The U.S. economy expanded modestly in 2011 and 2012, continuing the slow recovery since the recession ended in mid-2009. The Bureau of Economic Analysis (BEA) estimates that real per capita personal income grew by 2.8 percent in 2011 and by 1.6 percent in 2012, leaving that income measure below its 2008 peak.[10] CBO expects that economic activity will continue to expand slowly in 2013 with growth in real gross domestic product (GDP) of just 1.4 percent, suggesting that sluggish growth in real per capita income will continue in 2013.

Changes in the Distribution of Income

The Census Bureau provides estimates, on the basis of data from the Current Population Survey (CPS), of what is called household money income. That income measure differs both from CBO's measure of before-tax income and from BEA's measure of personal income. The Census Bureau estimates that real mean household money income rose by 0.2 percent in both 2011 and 2012. The CPS data indicate that there was a decline in household income for all groups other than households in the top quintile.[11] Consequently, income as measured in the CPS became more unequal, with the share of income going to households in the top quintile rising by 0.7 percentage points. That shift mostly occurred in 2011; the distribution of income was little changed from 2011 to 2012.

The tabulations of individual income tax returns filed for 2011 and 2012 tell a different story. In contrast to the small increase in real mean household money income reported in the CPS, real mean adjusted gross income on tax returns declined by 1.4 percent from 2010 to 2011 but rose by 3.3 percent from

2011 to 2012, based on preliminary tabulations of tax returns filed in 2013.[12] The distribution of that income was little changed between 2010 and 2011, but in 2012 the share of income going to the top percentile rose appreciably, again based on preliminary tabulations of tax returns filed in 2013. However, in anticipation of higher tax rates potentially taking effect in 2013, higher-income taxpayers probably shifted significant amounts of income from 2013 into 2012, thus providing a temporary boost to the reported income of higher-income taxpayers in 2012. That boost for 2012 would come at the expense of income to be reported in 2013 and would give the appearance of rapid growth in income in 2012 followed by slow growth or by a decline in 2013, with all else being equal.

Average Federal Tax Rates for 2011 and 2012

Aggregate federal tax receipts can provide some indication of average federal tax rates, although there is not a direct correlation. In particular, CBO's measure of average tax rates is based on tax liabilities accrued in a year, regardless of when those liabilities are paid; by contrast, federal receipts measure taxes paid to the government in a year, regardless of when those liabilities are incurred.

Total federal tax revenue grew slowly relative to the size of the economy in 2011 and 2012. Receipts in fiscal year 2010 were 15.1 percent of GDP, matching the mark set in 2009 for the smallest share of GDP since 1950. They rebounded slightly in fiscal year 2011, to 15.4 percent of GDP, and rose further in fiscal year 2012, to 15.8 percent of GDP. Those increases were largely attributable to individual income taxes, partially offset by declines in payroll taxes (mainly because of the temporary 2 percentage-point reduction in the statutory Social Security tax rate). Those figures imply that average tax rates probably remained quite low by historical standards in 2011 and 2012.

Changes in Tax Rules for 2013

Tax rules in 2013 differ from those of 2010 in important ways:

- Several provisions affecting high-income taxpayers, originally enacted in EGTRRA and JGTRRA, were allowed to expire in 2013;

- The Making Work Pay tax credit expired at the end of 2010, and payroll tax rates that had been reduced in 2011 and 2012 were reset to their earlier levels in 2013; and
- New taxes for high-income taxpayers enacted in the Affordable Care Act took effect in 2013.

Tax rules in 2010 reflected the changes made in EGTRRA and in JGTRRA. The tax rules enacted in those laws, originally scheduled to expire at the end of 2010, involved lower tax rates on ordinary income, lower tax rates on capital gains realizations and dividends, an expanded 15 percent tax bracket and larger standard deduction for married couples, a larger exemption from the alternative minimum tax, and a larger child tax credit. Several provisions of ARRA that held down taxes also were in effect in 2010 and originally scheduled to expire at the end of that year: the Making Work Pay tax credit, the American Opportunity Tax Credit (a refundable credit for postsecondary education expenses), a lower earnings threshold for the refundability of the child tax credit, and expansions to the earned income credit.

The Tax Relief, Unemployment Insurance Reauthorization, and Job Creation Act of 2010 extended the provisions of EGTRRA and JGTRRA through 2012. It also extended most of the credits enacted by ARRA for two years, although the Making Work Pay tax credit was allowed to expire. For 2011, the law provided a one-year reduction in the employee's share of the Social Security payroll tax. That reduction—from 6.2 percent to 4.2 percent—was extended through 2012 by two subsequent laws, but it was not extended into 2013. The 2010 tax act also increased the exemption for the alternative minimum tax.

The American Taxpayer Relief Act of 2012, which was enacted in early January 2013, made permanent most of the major provisions of EGTRRA and JGTRRA— with some exceptions for higher-income taxpayers. Specifically, for taxable income in excess of $400,000 (individual filers) and $450,000 (married people filing jointly), the lower tax rates originally enacted in 2001 expired as scheduled and the top statutory tax rate of 39.6 percent was reinstated. The tax rate for long-term capital gains and dividends increased from 15 percent to 20 percent for those same high-income taxpayers, and the act reinstated limitations on the use of personal exemptions and itemized deductions for individual taxpayers whose adjusted gross income was above $250,000 ($300,000 for joint filers). The act also permanently limited the reach of the alternative minimum tax and extended through 2017 the ARRA tax credits that were in effect in 2012. The law did not extend the payroll tax rate reduction.

The Affordable Care Act contained two new surtaxes on high-income taxpayers that also took effect in 2013. The Medicare payroll tax rate was increased by 0.9 percent for earnings above $200,000 for individual filers ($250,000 for joint filers). In addition, a new 3.8 percent surtax was imposed on the lesser of a taxpayer's investment income (consisting of interest, dividends, capital gains, and certain passive business activity) and total income over a threshold ($200,000 for individual filers and $250,000 for joint filers). The act also created new subsidies for the purchase of health insurance through exchanges and an excise tax on certain health insurance plans with high premiums; however, because those provisions take effect in 2014 and 2018, respectively, they are not considered here.

Average Federal Tax Rates under 2013 Tax Rules

CBO estimated the effects of the new tax provisions on average federal tax rates by simulating tax liabilities under 2013 tax rules using reported 2010 incomes and making an adjustment for estimated aggregate income growth between 2010 and 2013.[13]

Two important caveats apply to interpretation of the analysis. First, the analysis does not account for shifts in the distribution of income that might occur between 2010 and 2013; they will not be known for some time. The further recovery of the economy might result in uneven income growth, which could affect the distribution both of income and of federal taxes. Additionally, taxpayers probably changed their behavior in various ways in response to the changes in tax rules in 2013. For example, higher-income taxpayers probably shifted income from 2013 to 2012 in anticipation of the scheduled tax increases. Such shifts represent temporary changes in income, so holding incomes fixed, as in the current analysis, better represents the long-term effects of the tax change than would including those shifts. Higher-income taxpayers may also have reduced their income in permanent ways because of the tax increases, and holding incomes fixed would then overstate the increase in taxes. Second, CBO considered only the major changes to the individual income and payroll taxes and did not incorporate minor changes to those taxes or changes to the corporate income, excise, or estate and gift taxes. The American Taxpayer Relief Act significantly modified estate and gift tax rules for 2013 relative to the rules specified for that year under prior law, increasing the exemption amount from $1 million to $5.25 million and reducing the top rate from 55 percent to 40 percent. Still, those modified rules impose higher taxes than the rules that were in place in 2010, when the estate tax was effectively repealed.

Table 4. Average Federal Tax Rates under 2010 and 2013 Tax Laws, by Income Group

	Average Tax Rate (Percent)		Estimated Change in Average Tax Rate (Percentage points)	Estimated Change in After-Tax Income (Percent)
Income Group	Actual Under 2010 Law	Estimated Under 2013 Law		
Lowest Quintile	1.5	3.1	1.6	-1.6
Second Quintile	7.2	8.2	1.0	-1.1
Middle Quintile	11.5	12.5	1.0	-1.1
Fourth Quintile	15.6	16.4	0.8	-1.0
Highest Quintile	24.0	25.5	1.5	-2.0
All Quintiles	18.1	19.4	1.3	-1.6
81st to 90th Percentiles	19.3	19.9	0.6	-0.8
91st to 95th Percentiles	21.6	21.9	0.3	-0.4
96th to 99th Percentiles	24.9	25.2	0.3	-0.4
Top 1 Percent	29.4	33.6	4.2	-5.9

Source: Congressional Budget Office.

Notes: CBO estimated average federal tax rates for 2013 by simulating tax liabilities under 2013 tax rules using reported 2010 incomes and making adjustments for aggregate income growth between 2010 and 2013. Thus, the 2013 estimates do not incorporate any changes in taxpayers' behavior in response to the changes in tax rules.

Average federal tax rates are calculated by dividing federal tax liabilities by before-tax income.

Before-tax income is the sum of market income and government transfers. Market income is composed of labor income, business income, capital gains, capital income (excluding capital gains), income received in retirement for past services, and other sources of income. Government transfers are cash payments and in-kind benefits from social insurance and other government assistance programs.

After-tax income is the sum of market income and government transfers, minus federal tax liabilities.

Federal taxes include individual and corporate income taxes, social insurance (or payroll) taxes, and excise taxes.

Income groups are created by ranking households by before-tax income. Quintiles (fifths) contain equal numbers of people; percentiles (hundredths) contain equal numbers of people as well.

For more detailed definitions of income, see Appendix A.

Also, the deduction under the individual income tax for the declining value of investment property relies in 2013 on a depreciation schedule that is less generous than the schedule in effect in the final three months of 2010. Under the 2013 rules, depreciation deductions would be smaller and taxable business income and taxes would therefore be larger than the amounts reflected in CBO's analysis.

Holding the distribution of income constant and thereby not incorporating any changes in taxpayers' behavior in response to the changes in tax rules, CBO estimates that the average federal tax rate for all taxpayers will be 1.3 percentage points higher under the 2013 tax rules (as just described) than under the 2010 tax rules (see Table 4). That increase is the equivalent of a 1.6 percent decline in average after-tax income, holding all else equal.

However, the changes in federal tax rates and after-tax income will not be uniform across the income distribution. Average federal tax rates will increase more at either end of the income distribution—and particularly at the upper end—than in the middle.

CBO estimates that the average tax rate for households in the top percentile will be 4.2 percentage points higher under 2013 law than it was in 2010, which is equivalent to a 5.9 percent decline in after-tax income. That increase will occur because of the increase in tax rates for the highest-income households because of the expiration of earlier rate reductions and because of the high-income surtaxes enacted in the Affordable Care Act. CBO also estimates that the average tax rate for households in the lowest quintile will be 1.6 percentage points higher under 2013 law than it was in 2010. That increase largely reflects the expiration of the Making Work Pay tax credit.

Increases in average tax rates will be smaller for households in the rest of the income distribution, CBO projects. Relative to their levels in 2010, average tax rates under 2013 law will be between 0.8 and 1.0 percentage points higher for households in the second through fourth quintiles, 0.6 percentage points higher for house-holds in the 81st through 90th percentiles, and 0.3 percentage points higher for households in the 91st through 99th percentiles. That pattern arises because higher-income groups received relatively smaller benefits from the Making Work Pay tax credit, and the expiration of previous tax reductions and imposition of surtaxes on high-income taxpayers under the Affordable Care Act will not raise taxes very much on income groups below the top percentile.

CBO estimates that, for most income groups, average federal tax rates under 2013 law will still be below average rates in 2007, the year before the recession began (see Figure 3 on page 4). That outcome reflects legislated changes in tax rules (some of ARRA's tax credits will still be in place in 2013) and the effects of the slow economic recovery.

Households in the top income percentile, however, will face an average rate that is much higher than the average rates were in the years immediately before the recession.

The American Taxpayer Relief Act allowed the expiration of many of the tax reductions that applied to that income group in the early and middle 2000s. Those reversals, coupled with the new surtaxes, will push the average federal tax rate for the top percentile to an estimated 33.6 percent, the highest since 1997.

APPENDIX A: METHODOLOGY

When it estimates distributions of household income and federal taxes, the Congressional Budget Office (CBO) draws on data from various sources and makes judgments about the best way to use those data.

Data Sources on Household Income

Information on household income for this analysis came from two primary sources: the Internal Revenue Service's Statistics of Income (SOI) and the Census Bureau's Current Population Survey (CPS). The core data came from the SOI, a nationally representative sample of individual income tax returns that has increased from roughly 90,000 returns around 1980 to more than 300,000 returns in recent years.

CBO used the full Individual Income Tax file, which is more detailed than the public-use version of the file. The agency supplemented those data with data from the CPS's Annual Social and Economic Supplement; those data identify demographic characteristics and income for a large sample of households.

Both the SOI and the CPS lack important information needed for estimating and comparing after-tax household income over time. The SOI does not include information about people who do not file federal tax returns, and it does not report all income from government cash transfer programs. It also offers no information on the receipt of in-kind transfers and benefits, and it is organized by tax filing unit rather than by household. The CPS lacks detailed information on high-income households, it does not report capital gains, it underreports other income from capital, and it lacks information on the deductions and adjustments necessary to compute taxes.

Together, however, the two sources can form a relatively complete picture. To overcome limitations in each source of data, CBO statistically matched SOI records to corresponding CPS records on the basis of demographic characteristics and income. Each pairing resulted in a new record that took on the demographic characteristics of the CPS record and the income reported in the SOI. (Some types of income—certain transfers and in-kind benefits, for example—appear only in the CPS; their values were drawn directly from the CPS.)

Because some households are not required to file tax returns, the SOI does not have data on every household in the nation. To create a sample that was representative of the entire population, once all SOI records were matched to CPS records, the remaining CPS records were recorded as nonfiling households and their income values were taken directly from the CPS. CBO then estimated the tax liability for each record.

Allocation of Taxes to Households

CBO allocated individual income taxes and the employee's share of payroll taxes to the households paying those taxes directly. The agency also allocated the employer's share of payroll taxes to employees because employers appear to pass on their share of payroll taxes to employees by paying lower wages than they would otherwise pay.[1] Therefore, CBO also added the employer's share of payroll taxes to households' earnings in calculating before-tax income.

CBO allocated excise taxes to households according to their consumption of taxed goods and services (such as gasoline, tobacco, and alcohol). Excise taxes on intermediate goods, which are paid by businesses, were attributed to households in proportion to their overall consumption. CBO assumed that each household's spending on taxed goods and services was the same as that reported in the Bureau of Labor Statistics' Consumer Expenditure Survey for a household with comparable income and other characteristics.

Far less agreement exists about how to allocate corporate income taxes (and taxes on capital income generally). In this analysis, CBO allocated 75 percent of corporate income taxes to owners of capital in proportion to their income from interest, dividends, adjusted capital gains, and rents.[2] The agency used capital gains scaled to their long-term historical level, given the size of the economy and the tax rate that applies to them, rather than actual capital gains, so as to smooth out large year-to-year variations in the total amount of gains realized. CBO allocated the remaining 25 percent of corporate income taxes to workers in proportion to their labor income.

Measures of Income

This analysis uses three measures of household income: market income; market income plus government transfers (before-tax income); and market income plus government transfers, minus federal tax liabilities (after-tax income).

Market income includes the following components:

- *Labor Income.* Cash wages and salaries, including amounts allocated by employees to 401(k) plans; employment-based health insurance premiums; the employer's share of Social Security, Medicare, and federal unemployment insurance payroll taxes; and the share of corporate income taxes borne by workers.
- *Business Income. Net* income from businesses and farms operated solely by their owners, partnership income, and income from S corporations.
- *Capital Gains.* Profits realized from the sale of assets, excluding increases in the value of assets that have not been realized through sales.[3]
- *Capital Income Excluding Capital Gains.* Taxable and tax-exempt interest, dividends paid by corporations (but not dividends paid by S corporations, which are considered part of business income), positive rental income, and the share of corporate income taxes borne by owners of capital.
- *Other Income.* Income received in retirement for past services or from other sources.

Government transfers consist of cash payments from Social Security, unemployment insurance, Supplemental Security Income, Temporary Assistance for Needy Families (and its predecessor, Aid to Families with Dependent Children), veterans' programs, workers' compensation, and state and local government assistance programs. Such transfers also include the value of in-kind benefits: Supplemental Nutrition Assistance Program vouchers (popularly known as food stamps); school lunches and breakfasts; housing assistance; and energy assistance and benefits provided by Medicare, Medicaid, and the Children's Health Insurance Program. Health care benefits are measured using the Census Bureau's estimates of the average cost to the government of providing those benefits.[4]

Adjusting Income for Differences among Households

CBO used the household as the unit of analysis for this report. A household consists of the people who share a housing unit, regardless of their relationship to one another. The presumption is that households make joint economic decisions, although that might not be true in all cases (such as in a group house, for example). A household can consist of more than one taxpaying unit, such as a married couple living with an adult child.

Households with identical income also differ in ways that bear on their economic status. A larger household generally needs more income to support a given standard of living than a smaller one does. However, economies of scale in some types of consumption—housing, in particular—can mean that two people generally do not need twice the income to live as well as one person who lives alone. Therefore, to rank households by their standard of living, it is probably appropriate to divide household income by an adjustment factor that is between 1 (which would result only in household income and would not capture the greater needs of larger households) and the number of people in the household (which would produce household income per capita and would not capture the benefits of shared consumption). CBO chose to adjust for household size by dividing household income by the square root of the number of people in the household, counting adults and children equally.[5] Households were then ranked by adjusted income and grouped into quintiles of equal numbers of people. Because household sizes vary, different quintiles generally have slightly different numbers of households.

Adjusting the income for other differences in circumstances that affect a household's standard of living also could be desirable. For example, the prices of goods and services vary geographically, and households can incur different costs associated with working—for commuting and child care expenses, for example—depending on how many members are employed. CBO did not adjust for those additional differences.

Supplemental data tables, available online, show household income and average federal tax rates for three types of households: those with members under age 18 (households with children), those headed by a person age 65 or older and with no members under age 18 (elderly childless households), and all others (nonelderly childless households).[6] The tables group households into quintiles by position in the income distribution across the full population, not by distribution within each type of household, so each type of household is not evenly spread across the income quintiles.

APPENDIX B: VARIATION WITHIN INCOME GROUPS

This report analyzes average income and average federal tax rates for various subgroups of the U.S. population. Within each subgroup there are substantial variations, both in income and in average federal tax rates, for several reasons. Almost all of the differences in average payroll tax rates result from differences among households in the share of income from earnings, for example, but the variation in average individual income tax rates is affected both by the composition of income and by other factors, such as family structure, preferences in the tax code, and the progressive rate structure.

Before-Tax Income

For this study, the Congressional Budget Office (CBO) divided U.S. households into five groups on the basis of income, adjusted for household size. Each quintile (one-fifth of the population) consists of more than 25 million households and covers a fairly wide range of income and a smaller but still considerable range of income adjusted for household size (see Table B-1).[1] For households in the lowest income quintile, the size-adjusted annual income is between zero and $23,200. A one-person household with income within that range would fall into the lowest quintile, as would a four-person household with income below $46,500. The second and middle quintiles cover narrower ranges of size-adjusted income, and the range of the fourth quintile is roughly equal in size to that of the lowest income quintile.

Table B-1. Minimum Before-Tax Income for Different Income Groups, by Household Size, 2010 (Dollars)

						Percentiles Within the Highest Quintile			
Household Size	**Lowest Quintile**	**Second Quintile**	**Middle Quintile**	**Fourth Quintile**	**Highest Quintile**	**81st to 90th Percentiles**	**91st to 95th Percentiles**	**96th to 99th Percentiles**	**Top 1 Percent**
One-Person Household	0	23,200	35,700	51,100	75,700	75,700	103,500	139,100	306,900
Two-Person Household	0	32,900	50,500	72,300	107,100	107,100	146,400	196,700	434,000
Four-Person Household	0	46,500	71,400	102,200	151,500	151,500	207,100	278,200	613,800
Memorandum:									
Income Adjusted for Household Size	0	23,200	35,700	51,100	75,700	75,700	103,500	139,100	306,900

Source: Congressional Budget Office.

Notes: Before-tax income is the sum of market income and government transfers. Market income is composed of labor income, business income, capital gains, capital income (excluding capital gains), income received in retirement for past services, and other sources of income. Government transfers are cash payments and in-kind benefits from social insurance and other government assistance programs.

Income groups are created by ranking households by before-tax income. Quintiles (fifths) contain equal numbers of people; percentiles (hundredths) contain equal numbers of people as well.

For more detailed definitions of income, see Appendix A.

The ranges of income represented by the subgroups of the top quintile are much larger, however. And the before-tax income of the top percentile—more than 1 million households—ranges from $306,900 to hundreds of millions of dollars.

Average Federal Tax Rates

Different households within each quintile can have different average federal tax rates for any of several reasons, including the size of the household, the composition of income, and the amount claimed in tax-deductible expenses. To examine the variation of federal tax rates within quintiles, CBO first calculated the average tax rate for each household in its sample by dividing each household's federal tax liability by its income. CBO then tabulated the range of average individual income tax rates and payroll tax rates for households in each quintile in 2010. A comparable tabulation for corporate income tax rates or excise tax rates would not be meaningful because CBO's methods for allocating those taxes to households were not designed to capture the full range of variation in them.[2]

Payroll Tax Rates

For most workers, payroll taxes constitute a flat percentage of earnings (income from wages and self-employment). Therefore, most of the variation in average payroll tax rates arises because households derive different shares of their income from earnings. However, some variation in payroll taxes occurs because some workers have earnings above the maximum taxable amount for Social Security that are therefore not subject to the Social Security tax and some employed people are exempt from participating in Social Security or Medicare and therefore do not pay those taxes.

CBO examined the distribution of payroll tax rates in each quintile by ranking households from the lowest to the highest payroll tax rate. Within the lowest income quintile, the median rate is 8.8 percent—that is, half of all households have payroll tax rates above 8.8 percent and half have rates below (see the top panel of Figure B-1). In that group, the average payroll tax rate at the --10th percentile of the payroll tax distribution is zero, because at least 10 percent of households in the lowest quintile have no earnings and thus no payroll tax liability. The rate at the 90th percentile of the distribution is a little above 14 percent—about the rate for a household whose income is from earnings alone.[3] Because most households in the lowest quintile have some income from earnings and some from other sources, their payroll tax rates fall between zero and 14 percent. Within the lowest quintile, the average payroll tax rate at the 25th percentile is 2 percent and the rate at the 75th percentile is 13 percent.

In the other income quintiles, the variation in average payroll tax rates between the 10th and 90th percentiles is about the same as in the lowest quintile. In each quintile, a household in the 10th percentile of the rate distribution has an average payroll tax rate near zero, implying no earnings, and a household in the 90th percentile has a payroll tax rate between 13 percent and 14 percent, implying that the household's income is almost exclusively from earnings. But the payroll tax rate at the 25th percentile is higher for the fourth quintile and the highest quintile because fewer households in those groups have very low shares of income represented by earnings.

Individual Income Tax Rates

The individual income tax is more complex than the payroll tax, and average tax rates within a quintile can vary for any of several reasons, among them the following:

- *Income Composition.* Some forms of income, such as most transfer payments and compensation in the form of employment-based health insurance, are exempt from taxation. Some other forms of income, such as dividends and capital gains, are taxed at lower rates than ordinary income.
- *Tax Preferences.* In many cases, taxpayers can subtract state and local taxes, contributions to charity, mortgage interest on owner-occupied housing, and certain other expenses from their taxable income. The tax rate can be much lower for people with large deductions than it is for people who have about the same income but smaller deductions.
- *Family Structure.* The tax system makes adjustments for family size, through such provisions as personal exemptions and separate tax schedules for single, married, and head-of-household filers. Eligibility for the earned income tax credit and child tax credit depend on the presence of children (although taxpayers without children who meet certain age requirements can qualify for a small earned income tax credit).

- *Amount of Income.* Because individual income tax rates generally increase with income, households with income near the top of the range for a given quintile will tend to have higher tax rates than those with income near the bottom of that range.

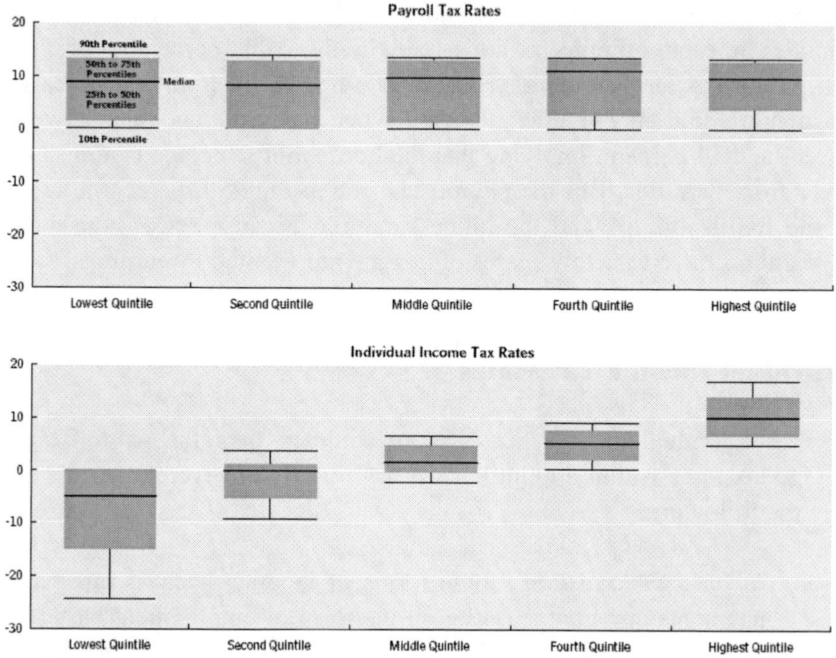

Source: Congressional Budget Office.

Notes: Average federal tax rates are calculated by dividing federal tax liabilities by before-tax income.

Before-tax income is the sum of market income and government transfers. Market income is composed of labor income, business income, capital gains, capital income (excluding capital gains), income received in retirement for past services, and other sources of income. Government transfers are cash payments and in-kind benefits from social insurance and other government assistance programs.

Federal taxes include individual and corporate income taxes, social insurance (or payroll) taxes, and excise taxes.

Income groups are created by ranking households by before-tax income. Quintiles (fifths) contain equal numbers of people. For more detailed definitions of income, see Appendix A.

Figure B-1. Distribution of Average Federal Tax Rates, by Income Group, 2010; (Percent).

CBO examined the distribution of income tax rates in each quintile by ranking households from the lowest to the highest income tax rate. There is more variation in income tax rates than in payroll tax rates in the lowest income quintile, less variation in the middle three quintiles, and about the same amount of variation in the highest quintile.

Within the lowest income quintile, the median individual income tax rate is -5 percent (see the bottom panel of Figure B-1).[4] A span of 24 percentage points separates the 10th from the 90th percentile of the rate distribution, with the average rate at the 10th percentile equal to -24 percent and the average rate at the 90th percentile equal to zero. The difference in rates between the 25th and 75th percentiles is 15 percentage points. The earned income tax credit and other refundable credits account for most of the variation in individual income tax rates: Households with children and low earnings are eligible for earned income tax credits (which often are larger than the regular income taxes owed), whereas other low-income households are either not eligible for those credits or are eligible for much smaller credits (because they have no earnings or have no qualifying children) but still owe no income tax.

The variation in average tax rates is much smaller in the second income quintile, where there is a separation of 13 percentage points between the 10th and 90th percentiles of the average rate distribution and a separation of 4 percentage points between the 25th and 75th percentiles. Eligibility for refundable credits is still a significant factor affecting income tax rates in the second quintile, so large numbers of households face negative average rates. There is even less variation in tax rates in the middle and fourth quintiles: The 10th and 90th percentiles are separated by 9 percentage points, and the 25th and 75th percentiles are separated by just 4 percentage points. In those income groups, eligibility for credits is much less important; most of the difference in rates arises from different shares of income stemming from taxable sources and differences in the amounts taken in itemized deductions.

There is more variation in the highest income quintile— in which 12 percentage points separate the 10th and 90th percentiles, and 6 percentage points separate the 25th and 75th percentiles—than there is in the middle and fourth quintiles. The variation in the highest income quintile is affected by two additional factors. First, the progressive rate schedule increases the variation in tax rates in the top quintile because of the wide range of incomes represented in that group. (The minimum household income for that group is $75,700, but the highest incomes are in the hundreds of millions of dollars.) Second, the tax rates some households in the top quintile face are lower than those faced by others because more of their income is in the form of dividends and capital gains, which are taxed at lower rates than ordinary income.

End Notes

[1] Information on definitions of income, the allocation of taxes, and the ranking of households is in "Notes and Definitions" at the front of this report.

[2] The Affordable Care Act comprises the Patient Protection and Affordable Care Act and the health care provisions of the Health Care and Education Reconciliation Act of 2010.

[3] See Congressional Budget Office, *The Distribution of Household Income and Federal Taxes, 2008 and 2009* (July 2012), www.cbo.gov/publication/43373, and *Trends in the Distribution ofHousehold Income Between 1979 and 2007* (October 2011), www.cbo.gov/publication/42729. Supplemental data for this report present estimates for the 1979–2010 period. See Congressional Budget Office, *The Distribution of Household Income and Federal Taxes, 2010* (December 2013), www.cbo.gov/ publication/44604.

[4] In a recent study, CBO analyzed the distribution of a slightly larger set of taxes as well as most federal spending. See Congressional Budget Office, *The Distribution of Federal Spending and Taxes in 2006* (November 2013), www.cbo.gov/publication/ 44698.

[5] Income measured over several years is more equally distributed than is income for a single year, although only modestly so. See Congressional Budget Office, *Effective Tax Rates: Comparing Annual and Multiyear Measures* (January 2005), www.cbo.gov/ publication/ 16212.

[6] In the federal budget, the refundable portion of income tax credits is counted as an outlay. In fiscal year 2010, the revenues collected from individual income taxes (which do not count the refundable portion of those tax credits) constituted a slightly larger share of gross domestic product (6.1 percent) than the revenues collected from payroll taxes (5.8 percent).

[7] For more discussion of the distribution of the corporate income tax, see Congressional Budget Office, *The Distribution of Household Income and Federal Taxes, 2008 and 2009* (July 2012), www.cbo.gov/publication/43373.

[8] Because of the complexity of estimating state and local taxes for individual households, this report considers federal taxes only. Researchers' conclusions differ about whether state and local taxes are, on net, regressive, proportional, or slightly progressive, but most agree that state and local taxes are far less progressive than federal taxes. For estimates, see Andrew Chamberlain and Gerald Prante, *Who Pays Taxes and Who Receives Government Spending? An Analysis of Federal, State, and Local Tax and Spending Distributions, 1991–2004,* Working Paper 1 (Tax Foundation, March 2007), http://tinyurl.com/lxzt6x6; and Carl Davis and others, *Who Pays? A Distributional Analysis of the Tax Systems in All 50 States*, 3rd ed. (Institute on Taxation and Economic Policy, November 2009), www.itep.org/state_reports /whopays.php.

[9] CBO chose 1979 as a starting point for the analysis because it is the earliest year for which the Census Bureau provides consistent estimates for some measures of income. However, the beginning and end points of the analysis, 1979 and 2010, were quite different in terms of overall economic activity; 1979 was an economic peak year right before a recession, whereas in 2010 a slow economic recovery had just begun.

[10] BEA's measures of income are different from those used by CBO. Personal income, as defined by BEA, is the income that people receive in return for their provision of labor, land, and

capital used in current production plus net current transfer payments that they receive from business and government.

[11] See Carmen DeNavas-Wilt, Bernadette D. Proctor, and Jessica C. Smith, *Income, Poverty, and Health Insurance Coverage in the United States: 2012* (Census Bureau, September 2013), Table A-2, http://go.usa.gov/WpJh.

[12] Estimates for 2012 are based on a tabulation of tax returns processed through the end of July 2013 (see Internal Revenue Service, "Filing Season Statistics" [November 12, 2013], www.irs.gov/uac/Filing-Season-Statistics). Income is measured in the tabulations as adjusted gross income, but that measure omits several nontaxable sources of income—such as employment-based health insurance and payments from the Supplemental Nutrition Assistance Program—that CBO includes in its measure of before-tax income.

[13] The analysis simulated taxes under 2013 tax rules by deflating tax parameters in 2013 by the estimated nominal rate of per capita income growth between 2010 and 2013 (approximately 7 percent). CBO then applied those adjusted tax parameters to 2010 incomes. The observed changes in tax rates thus capture both the effects of changes in tax law and a small amount of "bracket creep" to the extent that incomes were estimated to grow faster than inflation-indexed tax parameters.

End Notes for Appendix A

[1] That allocation reflects a consensus among economists. See Don Fullerton and Gilbert E. Metcalf, "Tax Incidence," in Alan J. Auerbach and Martin Feldstein, eds., *Handbook of Public Economics* (Elsevier, 2002), vol. 4, pp. 1787–1872.

[2] For a more detailed discussion of CBO's methodology for allocating corporate taxes, see Congressional Budget Office, *The Distribution of Household Income and Federal Taxes, 2008 and 2009* (July 2012), www.cbo.gov/publication/43373.

[3] CBO measures capital gains when the income is realized, partly based on the availability of data and partly to use the same accounting framework to measure income and taxes (which are levied on realized capital gains). Various researchers have measured capital gains as they accrue, on the basis of assets held by households at different income levels, but those researchers have reached disparate conclusions about the effect of accrued capital gains on levels and trends in income inequality, depending in large part on their assumptions about the rate of return on assets. See, for example, Timothy M. Smeeding and Jeffrey P. Thompson, *Recent Trends in the Distribution of Income: Labor, Wealth and More Complete Measures of Well Being*, Working Paper 225 (University of Massachusetts, June 2010), http://tinyurl.com/qd8qrxx; and Philip Armour, Richard V. Burkhauser, and Jeff Larrimore, *Levels and Trends in United States Income and Its Distribution: A Crosswalk From Market Income Towards a Comprehensive Haig-Simons Income Approach*, Working Paper 19110 (National Bureau of Economic Research, June 2013), www.nber.org/papers/ w19110.

[4] For more details on the method for valuing health care benefits, see Congressional Budget Office, *The Distribution of Household Income and Federal Taxes, 2008 and 2009* (July 2012), www.cbo.gov/publication/43373.

[5] That adjustment implies that each additional person increases a household's needs but does so at a decreasing rate. For example, a household consisting of a married couple with two children and an income of $80,000 would have an adjusted income of $40,000 ($80,000/'14) and would have the equivalent economic ranking of a single person with an

income of $40,000 or of a childless married couple with an income of $56,600 ($56,600/'12 is almost $40,000). See Constance F. Citro and Robert T. Michael, eds., *Measuring Poverty: A New Approach* (National Research Council, 1995), www.nap.edu/catalog.php?record_id=4759.

[6] The tables present estimates for the 1979–2010 period. See Congressional Budget Office, *The Distribution of Household Income and Federal Taxes, 2010* (December 2013), www.cbo.gov/ publication/44604.

End Notes for Appendix B

[1] Appendix A describes CBO's method for adjusting for household size.

[2] CBO allocated corporate income taxes in proportion to households' income from labor and capital, and the agency allocated excise taxes by assuming that each household's spending on taxed goods and services was the same as that reported in the Bureau of Labor Statistics' Consumer Expenditure Survey for a household with comparable income and other characteristics. In both cases, CBO's method allows for no additional variation in the amount of such taxes from one household to another.

[3] For a household with income only from earnings, CBO would add the employer's share of payroll taxes to those earnings, raising that amount by 7.65 percent. That household's payroll taxes would equal 15.3 percent of cash wages (after subtracting the employer's share of the payroll tax), for an average rate of 14.2 percent (15.3 divided by 1.0765).

[4] A negative rate indicates that refundable tax credits exceed income tax liability before those credits are applied.

INDEX

#

A

B

C

L

M

N

P

R

S

T

U

V

W